FRANCESCO'S
VENICE

BBC
BOOKS

FRANCESCO'S
VENICE

FRANCESCO DA MOSTO

PHOTOGRAPHS BY JOHN PARKER

Dedicated to all my family,
both living and long dead.

INTRODUCTION

One of my very earliest memories is of looking at the vast da Mosto family tree with its intriguing sea of names. As stories were related to me throughout childhood I grew to realize that our past, as that of one of the oldest families in Venice, is inextricably intertwined with the city's.

Founded in the last years of the Roman Empire or even earlier, Venice has an extraordinary history: of the resource-fulness that enabled the first settlers to create a city on water; of trade and exploration, supported by naval prowess and strategic warfare; and of artistic and architectural brilliance. Rather than attempt an exhaustive account I have built up, on a broad cultural and historical framework, a picture of the city through the centuries. And into this narrative I have woven the experiences of my own forebears. Inevitably not everyone associated with Venice could be mentioned in these pages, and what you are about to read comes from research into family papers as well as a huge number of books that have been written about my city and to which, I hope, many readers will turn in due course.

I have tried to enter into the lives of people who could help me describe the long evolution of this city, born on marshlands in a lagoon where there was nothing except birds, fish and mud, but where the savages of mainland Europe would never be able to follow them. Delving into family records I found remarkable ancestors in every period of Venice's long history and in the most disparate circumstances. Some achieved high office in the service of the state, although no one was ever a doge, nor does it seem that anyone ever put himself forward for election. A Renier da Mosto came closest in about 1300 – but perhaps he was lucky, since the successful candidate, Marin Falier, was beheaded a year later! There were also navigators and men of action, as well as scholars, courtesans and businessmen. And, as in all families, there were delinquents, black sheep and failures.

Venice is the only truly amphibious city in the world, a former trading crossroads between East and West, whose mingled influences are reflected in its language, art, traditions and people. The city still functions thanks to its closeness to the forces of nature and even in the twenty-first century

it is curiously modern, as one of the oldest examples of 'sustainable development'. A dense urban environment that virtuously maintains the human scale, its transport infrastructure based on the canal network, it still lives to the rhythm of the tides, which help maintain ecological balance in the lagoon. Any threat to nature would be a threat to Venice.

My career in architecture and the film industry has also connected me with the rich cultural and architectural heritage of Venice, and when I was approached by the BBC in 2003 to present a television series on the city I was delighted by the opportunity. I am delighted, too, that John Parker has taken such fabulous photographs to record the wonderful Venetian buildings, as well as the city's mysterious waterways and some little-known but fascinating slices of life. His pictures reveal the history, outstanding craftsmanship and vibrancy of this unique city that has been, and remains, the inspiration for so much art, ingenuity and passion.

Francesco da Mosto

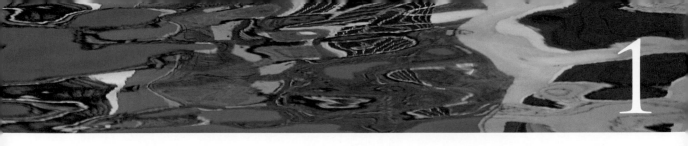

1

WATER

FROM THE WATERS TO THE CITY

Legend has it that St Mark, after founding the patriarchy of Aquileia in north-eastern Italy on behalf of St Peter, set sail for Rome but was driven by a storm into what is now the lagoon of Venice, where his boat ran aground on one of its deserted, marshy islands. The exhausted Evangelist, saved from the fury of the elements, had a dream in which he saw an angel who addressed these words to him:

Peace be to you, Mark, my Evangelist, and know that one day your bones will rest here. You have a long life ahead of you, Evangelist of God, and many trials to bear in Christ's name. But after your death the faithful people of this land will build a wonderful city here and will prove worthy to possess your body. You will be venerated honourably.

When, in the ninth century, the saint's body was stolen from its burial-place in Alexandria and brought to what had by then become the city of Venice, the prophecy was held to have come true. The symbol of St Mark has always been the lion, with its connotations of power, justice and divine providence. It was adopted by the Venetians, and this image, sometimes winged, often holding a book or scroll, either sculpted anew or brought as booty from elsewhere, is still to be found all over Venice. But where did the people who founded the city of St Mark's vision come from?

In the third century AD the Roman Empire started its long, steady decline. Its vast size made it difficult to govern, and some of the more distant provinces, such as those in the Middle East and the

Opposite: The entrance to the Grand Canal that runs through the heart of Venice and that allows the city to breathe, thanks to the rhythm of the tides.

Balkans, were gradually over-run by marauding tribes from the East. In the
late fourth century the empire was divided into two: the Western Empire was
ruled from Milan, briefly, and then Ravenna, and the Eastern Empire from
Constantinople (the former Greek city of Byzantium). Shortly afterwards
Italy itself was invaded by one of these warlike tribes, the Visigoths from the
North, who in 410 reached Rome and sacked it. The Western Empire hung
on for a few decades more, but it was doomed; it was the self-appointed
task of the Byzantine emperors to reconquer Italy and restore Christianity,
and to this end they regarded all regions of Italy, not only those occupied
by the invaders, as part of their domain.

Wave upon wave of invaders ravaged the peninsula. The roads that
were the pride of the Roman Empire, and which had enabled it to expand
and to defend itself, now hastened its end, facilitating the swift, violent
raids of the 'barbarians', among the most bloodthirsty of whom was Attila,
Scourge of God, King of the Huns. His nomadic horsemen of Turko-
Mongolian stock fed on meat warmed beneath their saddles, and were
armed with primitive weapons such as nooses, nets, and bows and arrows
made of horn. Clustering together in small bands, as liable to fight among
themselves as to unite against an enemy, they were fearfully described as 'wild
animals', 'two-legged beasts' and 'half-men who eat their own elders and
drink their blood'. Against this background of violence and destruction,
many people in Italy became refugees.

In the northeast a small mainland community who had lived by fishing and producing salt, and may have included my own forebears (see page 15), sought safety among the marshy islets of the Venetian lagoon, part of a delta formed by the River Po and other waterways. They built settlements among the inaccessible islands. Fanciful theories on the ancient origins of these people abound. A manuscript from the middle of the second millennium gives us a description of the Venetians: 'The origin and lineage of the true and most worthy Venetians and their families come from the most noble and ancient Trojan lords and barons and peoples, who fled from their most noble and great city of Troy, destroyed and burned by the Greeks in the year 4209 from the Creation of the World, with their families, their goods and their ships.' Patriotically inspired Italian chroniclers claim that they descend from the ancient *Henetoi*, as Homer calls them, which is Greek for 'praiseworthy'. The Heneti, or Veneti, are said to have brought Mycenean and Ancient Greek civilization to the primitive tribes of Italy, teaching them the arts and skills of navigation, agriculture, weaving, the alphabet, archi-tecture, metalwork, animal breeding and sheep farming. Latin and Greek sources assert that they came from Paphlagonia, a region near the Black Sea. Other sources point to Illyria, on the eastern shore of the Adriatic.

Below: Known as a *bilancia*, this type of fishing net has been used for centuries. The wooden stucture is much the same as original *casoni*, the homes of the first lagoon inhabitants.

The *casoni* or houses of these first inhabitants of the lagoon were probably little more than rude huts put up in a hurry, using whatever was locally available, by desperate refugees. The dwellings were made from woven osier branches, and had small windows and earthen floors with fireplaces in the middle, like the constructions still to be found in the lagoons of Grado and Caorle, east along the coast from modern Venice. There were no flues to remove the smoke so the inhabitants had to leave the door open in order to breathe, see and talk. However, the smoke kept away the mosquitoes and, being oily, clung to the osiers, making them more waterproof. Gradually, as more refugees fled the barbarian onslaughts, bricks made from lagoon mud began to replace the original building materials and the constructions became more sophisticated.

Before building a *cason*, each family had to choose a sufficiently high patch of marshland, then consolidate and raise it, excavating the soil round about; in this way they created a moat-like canal, isolating the house and its land from the surrounding marshland. This long ditch, dug deep into the mud, contained water even at low tide so that the fishermen could always use their boats. The soil of the hut was protected from erosion by a stockade of interwoven osier branches – an early model for the later *fondamente* (canal banks) that characterize Venice today.

Venice, then, was created from nothing by free people on islands in an empty wilderness. This is the essence of the city's unwillingness to be subject to anything or to anybody. Cassiodorus, Prefect of Ravenna and the surrounding region under Theodoric the Ostrogoth, Byzantine ruler of Italy at the close of the fifth century, deeply admired the early, *casoni*-dwelling Venetians, living 'like sea-birds, with your homes dispersed, like the Cyclades, across the surface of the water. The solidity of the earth on which they rest is secured only with osier and wattle; yet you do not hesitate to oppose so frail a bulwark to the wildness of the sea … All your energies are spent on your salt-fields; in them indeed lies your prosperity … For though there may be men who have little need of gold, yet none live who desire not salt … ' Even in those days the Venetians were well known as traders.

The nineteenth-century art critic and writer John Ruskin, who loved Venice, noted how a settlement begun in adversity proved to have enduring and extraordinary advantages: 'Had deeper currents divided their islands, hostile navies would again and again have reduced the rising city into servitude; had stronger surges beaten their shores, all the richness and refinement of the Venetian architecture must have been exchanged for the walls and bulwarks of an ordinary sea-port. Had there been no tide, as in other parts of the Mediterranean, the narrow canals of the city would have become noisome, and the marsh in which it was built pestiferous.'

Opposite: With my illustrious ancestor, Alvise da Mosto, a famous explorer who discovered the Cape Verde islands off the west coast of Africa in 1456 at the age of twenty-nine.

THE ORIGINS OF THE DA MOSTO FAMILY

MANUSCRIPTS INDICATE that my family moved to the Venetian lagoon in 454 with the arrival of Attila. An alternative version is that the family already lived in the Treviso area, as farmers and vine-growers, which may explain the name Mosto, which means 'must', the first state of the pressed grapes in the wine-making process; the family is said to have moved to the lagoon after the destruction of Treviso two centuries later by the Lombards. Others suggest that a branch of the 'illustrious and ancient' Cadamosto family from Lodi took shelter in Venice in 1158 after their homeland was laid waste by the Milanese. There may be some truth in this. In 1520 Davide Cadamosto of Lodi wrote an account of his journey to the Holy Land, in which he stated that in the solemn procession that always preceded embarkation, each pilgrim was accompanied by a Venetian nobleman. He happened to be assigned to a da Mosto who, on hearing his name and origin, greeted him with extraordinary affection, declaring that his family had come originally from Lodi. Whatever the truth of these accounts, the da Mosto family appears in Venice in documents of the twelfth century; and in 1297 it was included in the *Serrata del Maggior Consiglio* (Locking of the Great Council) as one of the 'new

families', thus legally becoming part of the Venetian patrician elite.

The da Mosto family, of course, goes further back than its connection with Venice. The earliest memorial inscription that I have found says in Latin:

BY DECREE OF THE DECURIONS, this was erected to Titus Mustius son of Caius Hostilius, belonging to the Fabia people, added to Fabritius, to

Augurinus and to the Medulla peoples, among the ex-tribunes by Emperor Caesar Nerva Augustus, praetor and curator of the pontifical treasury.

This takes us back to the first century AD, to the time when Jerusalem was destroyed by the Romans, Pompeii smothered by the lava of an erupting Vesuvius and Rome burned to the ground at the hand of its own Emperor, Nero.

But the magnificent city that Ruskin knew lay in the future. In the
sixth and seventh centuries the Venetian people were still living precariously,
even though the Byzantine Eastern Empire, based on Greek culture, was
enjoying a golden age: at this time the great church of St Sophia was
consecrated in Constantinople, and the splendid mosaics of Empress
Theodora and Emperor Justinian were laid in Ravenna's church of San
Vitale. Meanwhile, Byzantine missionaries stole silkworms from China
and silk became the monopoly of the Empire. This was also the time of
Mohammed, founder of Islam, whose Turkish adherents were to become
one of the Venetian Republic's chief rivals for hundreds of years.

And still the depredations of warring tribes from the East continued
in Italy. More people were driven to seek shelter in the lagoon after the
violent influx of a Germanic tribe, the Lombards. In 639, when the city of
Oderzo fell to them, the seat of the local Byzantine governor was moved
to Cittanova, renamed Heraclea, by the Emperor Heraclius. His name is
recorded in an inscription celebrating the foundation of the church of

Opposite: The interior
of the church of Santa
Maria Assunta in Torcello
testifies to early Byzantine
presence in Venice.
Above: Eastern-influenced
decorations and marble
floors adorn the church –
this mosaic of the Last
Judgement vividly depicts
sinners being sent to hell.

FISHING

FISH, IN PARTICULAR ANCHOVIES, sardines and mackerel, was for centuries the staple food for most of the inhabitants of the Adriatic coast. For the people of the lagoon the tide brought in daily swarms of such fish, as well as mullet, gilthead, sole, sea bass and eels.

Traditional practices still persist today. In the lagoon reed cages are fastened to the canal bottoms with poles, and the tide sweeps fish into their labyrinthine nets. The same system is used in autumn for eels, which are inveigled into large, round wooden tubs known as *vieri*; these are also used for keeping *moeche*, soft-shelled crabs that eat one another to survive.

Restrictions on fishing practices are as old as fishing in the lagoon. An ancient stone inscription, marking the minimum lengths at which different kinds of fish can be sold so as not to endanger their reproductive capacity, can still be seen at the Rialto fish market.

Santa Maria Assunta in Torcello in the northern lagoon, a building that sums up the spirit of the times. Its coloured marble and architecture evoke the distant East, while the great stone shutters recall the threat of barbarian invasions.

Although recognizing the dominion of the Eastern Empire, the Venetians enjoyed a considerable degree of independence from the earliest times, mainly thanks to their remoteness and isolation. In other respects their situation was similar to that of the major centres of Byzantine Italy, governed by locally elected leaders known as dukes, which in Venetian dialect became doges. The first doge of Venice – although this is not universally agreed – appears to have been Paoluccio Anafesto (Anafesto being the original surname of the Falier family, who figured large in Venetian politics for the next nine centuries). He is said to have been elected in 697 by the general assembly of the Venetians in Heraclea in an effort to end internal dissension and to defend themselves against the Lombards.

The only thing that the chroniclers tell us about Paoluccio's administration is that he settled the confines of Heraclea with the king of the Lombards, Liutprand, and had a dispute with the patriarch of Grado, the local bishop. Subsequently some of the dignitaries of the neighbouring town of Malamocco rebelled against him; they conquered Heraclea, set fire to it, and then apparently murdered him and his family.

To succeed Paoluccio, the Venetians chose Orso, 'a most noble Heraclean citizen'. His election took place as uprisings raged throughout Italy in response to an edict ordering the destruction of all holy images by the Eastern Emperor Leo III. This suggests that Orso's election may have been an initiative not of the people, but rather of the troops that had mutinied in Istria and maritime Venice against the emperor. At any rate, in 726 Orso became the first indisputable doge.

GREATER AUTONOMY, EXPANDING TRADE

In 742, under the leadership of Diodato, 'Master of the Soldiers', the seat of government was transferred from Heraclea to the island of Malamocco, a short distance from the present Malamocco, which lies on a slender strip of land that separates the lagoon from the sea. Here, safer from outside influence, the Venetians assembled to elect Diodato himself as doge; at the time he was viewed with favour by the Byzantines and received the title of *hypatos* or consul, which represented imperial authority and implied a certain autonomy. The extent of Byzantine influence on the Venetians and the language spoken by them is reflected in what can be traced of my own family name (see pages 15 and 23); the details I have unearthed, in Greek, Latin and Slav languages, all seem to interconnect.

Opposite: Fishing, one of Venice's oldest traditions, remains an important part of life for many Venetians, who pride themselves on their skill.

Autonomy was something the Venetians strove to increase, while being careful not to go too far. Their concern was not expansion or aggrandizement but unimpeded trade and the ability to defend themselves from pirates (and other invading enemies). Indeed, the move to Malamocco indicates a greater commitment to maritime commerce. Although Heraclea was situated on the edge of the lagoon, its economy was based on agriculture and other traditional terrestrial pursuits. Now, with activities centred on an island within the lagoon itself, the way was prepared for Venice's future as a sea power. As trade expanded in the Adriatic, river transport was equally important: the lagoon was linked to the great northern plain via the River Po, which the Venetians controlled by building castles on its banks.

Life in the duchy of the Venetians – landowners, merchants, sailors and farmers – continued undisturbed, hardly troubled even by the fall in 751 of Ravenna, the Byzantines' political and military centre for the control of the lagoons, to the Lombards. Then, towards the end of the eighth century, the Frankish conquest of the Lombard kingdom, followed by Charlemagne's coronation as emperor of the West in Rome in the year 800, put new pressures on the Venetians, who for their survival felt obliged to play a double game.

In 805 Doge Obelario and the Duke of Dalmatia, under the auspices of the patriarch of Grado, travelled to Aquisgrana (Aix-la-Chapelle, nowadays Aachen), the Frankish capital, and presented gifts to the Emperor Charlemagne; in return they obtained a form of acknowledgement of the independence of their territories provided they did not recognize Byzantine authority. The court of Constantinople regarded this as an affront: in 809 a powerful fleet easily broke through the feeble defences of the duchy of Dalmatia and then headed resolutely for the Venetian lagoon. Doge Obelario immediately surrendered, attributing all reponsibility for the crisis to the patriarch, who had meanwhile fled the land.

These were troubled years, with Venice torn between the two powerful clashing empires, lacerated also by internal factions and conspiracies, and vacillating in its policies. In 810, determined to reimpose sovereignty, Charlemagne sent his son Pepin, King of Italy, with a powerful naval force to occupy the northern Adriatic. Starting from Ravenna, Pepin attacked and conquered Dalmatia, and then turned towards the Venetian lagoon. He first attacked Chioggia, which he defeated although with heavy losses. Then he was brought to a halt before Malamocco, the seat of government, since all the Venetian defence forces were concentrated there. Meanwhile, for greater safety, a large number of refugees had made their way further into the lagoon, where the Castle of Olivolo defended the Rivoalto islands (*rivo alto* meaning 'high ground'; later the name would be contracted to the more familiar Rialto). The seat of power was now transferred to these islands. This marks the true birth of the city of Venice.

Previous spread: On the island of Burano the houses were painted in bright colours so that the fishermen could see their homes as they approached on their boats, even in the fog.

A NAME WITH ASSOCIATIONS

I LOOKED FOR THE ETYMOLOGY of my family name in the languages of the various places where it may have originated. In Ancient Greek inscriptions from the Athens region, the only word I found that could be associated with a person was *mustes*. The meaning changed depending on its spelling, *mustes* or *moustos*, but there remained a curious connection between the two words. *Mustes* referred to the ancient priests initiated in the Mysteries of Bacchus or Dionysius, the god of wine – made from *mosto*, grape must, which is what the second word, *moustos*, means. Perhaps these priests pre-pared magic potions for Dionysiac feasts, or took the potions them-selves like shamans in nocturnal rituals when religious and temporal powers were united. They may have been leaders or navigators of people who emigrated from Paphlagonia or Illyria to northern Italy, as Latin inscriptions have confirmed.

In Slavonic languages from the Balkans to Poland, from ancient Thrace invaded by the Slavs, to distant Dacia on the Caspian Sea, the word *most*, or variants of it, means 'bridge'. We all recall the image of the Roman bridge of Mostar, destroyed in the recent Balkan wars. Here in Venice the Rialto Bridge still has saints and madonnas at its base, since in former

times people needed to trust in God, or the supernatural, before crossing water. So 'bridge' could stand for a connection between the earthly and the unearthly, thus linking up with the Greek and Latin meanings in which wine may have been the shamans' magic potion.

We are not so far from the putative original name of the Venetians, the Heneti, which meant 'men of wine'. For my part, as a twenty-first-century da Mosto, I am perfectly comfortable with this association with the habitual *ombra*. *Ombra*, by the way, refers to the shade of St Mark's Campanile, where in past times wine was placed to keep cool, and is now the local term for a glass of wine.

Above: The Rialto Bridge is in the commercial and political heart of Venice. The saints and madonnas that are carved into its base hark back to a time when people needed spiritual help to build their bridges, which were seen as a force against nature.

Malaria stalled the Frankish fleet and army for several months. It was the time of year when the rivers were in full spate, and the influx of fresh water into the lagoon regenerated the populations of mosquitoes. This, in fact, was why the inhabitants of the northern lagoon, between Malamocco and Torcello, had gradually moved towards the Rivoalto islands and away from the river mouths. When, legend has it, the Frankish fleet eventually decided to enter the lagoon, they asked a woman for directions to the Rialto islands. 'Sempre diritto' – straight ahead – she replied, and the deep-keeled Frankish ships ran aground and were duly destroyed by the Venetians, who had swift, agile, shallow-bottomed lagoon craft and slaughtered the helpless Franks in their thousands. At that time the deeper channels were not marked, precisely so as to prevent enemies from penetrating the lagoon. The local fishermen and sailors, of course, knew how to navigate these tricky waters. The Venetians were to maintain this defensive strategy right up to the end of the Republic in 1797; indeed, had they not decided to surrender to Napoleon, his ships would have had problems, even though the Republic was then at its lowest ebb. Nowadays the countless bricole (poles) that mark the navigable channels are a very special feature of the Venetian lagoon; they vary in number, colour and shape according to a specific system of identification, and provide perches for the birds. And as for the notion of 'straight ahead', even today a typical Venetian, if asked directions by a typical tourist, tends to reply, 'sempre diritto', irrespective of destination.

Peace was signed between the two empires in 814: it guaranteed the territorial integrity of the duchy of the Venetians from Grado to Chioggia. As people began to settle in greater numbers around Rivoalto, geographically in the centre of the lagoon, Malamocco and Heraclea declined in importance, and even Torcello, which the Byzantines had termed emporion mega, began to feel the competition. Contemporary chronicles recount the splendour of the religious buildings, and it seems that daily life was becoming more luxurious, with fine furnishings and tableware. However, the women took a bath only once a month, perhaps this was because washing removed the defensive patina of grease, overlaid with perfumes, that kept them warm, or because fresh-water wells were still rare. These wells, vital for the supply of drinking-water, were excavated by private citizens in the campi (squares) and court-yards. The well-heads, carved from new stone or hollowed out of Roman columns, were the only visible part of an extremely complex system. Each of these wells consisted of a cistern about 5 metres (16½ feet) deep, with waterproof clay walls. At the centre of the cistern there was a brick conduit, with slits in the lower part. The cistern was partly filled with sand. Rain-water, channelled by drainage holes in the paving-stones up above, was collected in a tank close to the well and connected to it by pipes. Filtered

Opposite: An ancient well-head in the court-yard of Goldoni's house. Rainwater was collected via a system of drains. Larger palaces had their own wells, but most people drew their water from public wells in the campi (squares) and courtyards.

by the sand, the water rose up again into the well from where it could be drawn off.

After the seat of government had been moved to the Rivoalto, the Venetians elected as doge Agnello Partecipazio, a member of one of the 'tribune' families. At that time, maritime tribunes presided over small clusters of islands with their tiny populations and were charged with trying to impose order. The doge's family came from Heraclea; thanks to their successful *fondachi* (trading-posts), they owned great estates, with vineyards, marshlands, fields and mills in the hinterland of the lagoon, cattle, orchards, grazing land, forests and river transport, as well as a palace at the Rivoalto and numerous servants. It is from this line that the aristocratic Badoer family reputedly derive; their enormous wealth gave rise, in the late days of the Republic, to the expression '*pien come el Badoer*' (loaded like a Badoer).

Under Partecipazio's dogeship the first Venetian coin was struck, bearing the name of the Western Emperor, Lewis the Pious, which testifies to the influence of the Western Empire in maritime Venice. They had extensive commercial dealings; Venice enjoyed the same privileges with the Western Empire as it did with the Eastern, which was happy to leave the matter of trade to the Venetians. It is said that in 829 the emperor of Byzantium, Theophilus, gazing from the window of the Great Palace of Constantinople and observing a large merchant ship advancing slowly towards the port, asked who owned such a beautiful vessel. Being told that it was his own wife, the empress, he declared: 'God made me emperor, and you, woman, want to make me a sea captain!' and he had the ship and all its merchandise burned. Theophilus was demonstrating his compliance with the Roman law that prohibited noblemen from engaging in trade 'so that plebeians and merchants might carry out their business in greater tranquillity', as Alvise Zorzi writes in his book *Una Città, Una Repubblica, Un Impero Venezia 697–1797*. The Byzantine emperor confined himself to exacting heavy taxes.

In the mid-ninth century the islands that had been devastated by the Frankish invasion were repopulated, Heraclea was rebuilt under its former name of Cittanova, and the Rivoalto islands were systematically built up. The first Doge's Palace was erected, conceived as a fortress with thick walls, crenellated towers and drawbridges.

The Venetians were growing steadily more powerful through commerce and maritime activities rather than by increasing the size of their territory, as was the case with many other powers. They were now able to send ships to help the Byzantine Greek fleet in the struggle against the Muslim Saracens, who had invaded Sicily. But the most important event of the period, in 828, was the arrival in Venice of the body of St Mark the Evangelist.

The story goes that two Venetian merchants with ten cargo-laden ships were driven by the wind into the port of Alexandria. When they visited the church of St Mark where the saint's body was buried, they found the Greek priests who were its custodians in a state of agitation. The caliph of the Saracens had decided to build a palace near Babylon and had ordered the marble to be removed from all Christian churches for its decoration; the priests naturally feared their own church might be devastated and its relics profaned.

The two Venetians asked to be allowed to take the saint's body to Venice, promising the custodians great honours and generous recompense from the doge. But the priests were horrified – St Mark had been commanded to preach his Gospel here and they were terrified that his faithful followers would kill them if they were to let St Mark's body leave the church. Indeed, a man had recently been scourged for destroying a precious stone in the Temple in order to prevent its removal by the Muslims. The merchants were able to reassure the priests that it was in fact they who had the first claim to the saint's sermons, because St Mark first preached in the land of the Veneti, in Aquileia.

The Greek priests saw the sense in this and agreed to hand over the body, which lay wrapped in a silk shroud closed with numerous seals. Having removed the body of St Mark, they replaced it with that of St Claudian, cunningly managing to keep the seals unbroken. Suddenly a sweet perfume wafted from the body and spread throughout the city. This was the 'odour of sanctity' associated with relics, and people grew suspicious. Some of them ran to the church and opened the tomb, but they found the shroud still sealed. Meanwhile, in order to convey the Evangelist's body in secret to their ships the Venetians had wisely covered it in pork – anathema to Muslims, who may have checked their cargo. Among the many miracles said to have been performed on the journey to Venice, St Mark appeared one night to a monk in a vision, bidding him warn the sailors to lower the sails because a storm was due. At dawn they arrived safely in Dalmatia on the eastern Adriatic coast. Once in Venice, the holy relic was placed temporarily in a chapel alongside the Doge's Palace, until a church could be built that was worthy of it. Some other sources claim that the body was stolen and conveyed to Venice on the express orders of Doge Giustiniano Partecipazio, son of the previous Doge Partecipazio, to add political prestige and honour to his city's undoubted commercial status. There are also some who say, ironically perhaps, that the saint's body has only been borrowed, to be returned when the Basilica of St Mark is completed. This is why, even now, work on the church drags on year after year: as soon as restoration work finishes on one part of the building it immediately starts up again on another.

Left: Mosaics on the façade of St Mark's Basilica depict the arrival in Venice of the body of St Mark. Created in 1265, they show the original façade of the church, complete with the newly installed bronze horses.

WITH HIS BODY SAFELY IN CHRISTIAN VENICE, the Evangelist was proclaimed patron saint of the city, replacing the Greek Theodore – a clear indication of the Venetians' wish to shake off lingering Byzantine tutelage. The first church to house the relic was completed in 832, but in 976 was destroyed during a rebellion. The saintly Doge Pietro Orseolo I immediately had it rebuilt. As Venice continued to grow in wealth and power, the city was seized with a building frenzy and in the late eleventh century a new church was proposed. The sanctuary

THE BYZANTINE BASILICA OF ST MARK

of St Mark would become both a mausoleum and the private chapel of the doge, thus serving both a political and a religious function. Two magnificent buildings standing side by side, the Basilica of St Mark and the Doge's Palace, still symbolize to the world the power and achievement of the great city of Venice.

Although the balance of power between Venice and Byzantium was now reversed, in matters of taste the East still prevailed. In St Mark's Basilica, in particular, the city

continued to show a surprising fidelity to Byzantium, almost a curious desire to appropriate its culture. This continuity was to be seen above all in the use of mosaics, so typical of Byzantine art, and the persistent fashion for decoration against a gold background, as on the façade of the church.

Venice modelled the third St Mark's on two basilicas from imperial Byzantium: the Holy Apostles, which no longer exists, and St Sophia. The new Basilica, designed on the Greek-cross plan with a raised sanctuary to give space for a crypt, was consecrated in 1094 by Doge Vitale Falier. A bare brick structure with a cluster of low domes over the arms and the central crossing, it is

Previous pages: The façade of the Basilica, richly decorated with gold in the Byzantine style and the traditional symbols of Venice – St Mark and the winged lion. The lead domes were added in the thirteenth century.
Above: Detailed carvings representing the months of the year and signs of the zodiac.
Above right: Two of the Tetrachs – an example of fourth-century Afro-Egyptian art.
Opposite: The interior, richly decorated in the Byzantine style with gold and a marble floor.

predominantly Greek-Byzantine in style with some Arab and Gothic features.

Until the fifteenth century the outside was constantly changed, especially in the rich ornamentation of the façade.

All the external decoration visible today is relatively recent, with the exception of the thirteenth-century mosaics on the far left, *The Translation of the Body of St Mark*, which show the building before the Gothic features were added. Subsequent Gothic ornamentation over the arches gave an impression of extra height and harmonized with the new Doge's Palace. The slow process of decoration resulted in the amazing mixture of styles, but what is even more striking is the building's insistent orientalism. Many of the ornaments were acquired, or looted, from the East during trading trips, wars or crusades. For instance, the two pillars from Acre are examples of sixth-century Syriac art and were taken as trophies

following the Venetian victory over the Genoese in the thirteenth century; while the porphyry group of the Tetrarchs, inserted into the façade towards the Piazzetta, is an example of fourth-century Afro-Egyptian art.

Over time, each dome was covered by a second taller dome, a wooden structure coated with lead, crowned by a lantern with a gilded cross. The bricks, too, were overlaid with marble. On the main façade a double row of columns with capitals was added, also of fine marble from the East. Carved leaf-shapes, aedicules and pinnacles cavort above the large arches in Gothic exuberance. The main door was surrounded with bas-reliefs representing the trades of man and the signs of the zodiac.

The church is entered via a narthex, a point of transition between the outside, a great open space bathed in light, and the inside, a serene space in which the gloom contends with a golden glow. The interior reveals itself gradually, as you make your way over a marble floor embellished with twelfth-century mosaics in which figures of animals alternate with geometrical patterns – another testimonial to Byzantine influence. In front of the altar, where the fourteenth-century jewel-studded gold screen known as the Pala d'Oro gleams, is the iconostasis, a characteristic Eastern feature separating the main body of the church from the sanctuary. It is in red marble

with multi-coloured panels; above these are columns with capitals supporting the architrave, adorned with masterpieces of fourteenth-century Gothic sculpture by the Dalle Masegne brothers. The work of mosaic decoration continued over several centuries, and since its aim was to teach the illiterate the rudiments of religious history, the walls resemble an enormous illustrated Bible.

For me the Basilica is a strong religious symbol with personal meaning. It was in the crypt that I received my

First Communion and was later confirmed by the future Pope John Paul I. As a boy, I was filled with awe at the majesty and richness of the Basilica, overwhelmed by the glittering colours of the mosaics and elaborate marble floor patterns from unknown worlds. The crypt took me into its serene embrace as I received Communion, the sacrament that (so I had been taught) had existed among the first Christians who met in the Roman catacombs and shared their food and their life of sacrifice.

Right: Detail of the façade of St Mark's Basilica, with coloured marble sourced from all over the world.

Although the Saracens had not penetrated the Adriatic, Venice at this time was continually beset by conspiracies from within and external threats such as the Narentine pirates from Dalmatia, who plagued the seas round about. In 831 Obelario, the pro-Frank doge who had been exiled to Constantinople twenty years earlier, before Pepin's assault, managed to escape and landed with a number of armed followers near the old capital of Malamocco, his home town. The response from the current doge, Giovanni Partecipazio I, was immediate: Malamocco was laid waste and the would-be usurper taken prisoner and executed, his head being put on public display as a grim warning. But it was only a brief respite, for the other families, chafing against the high-handed ways of the Partecipazio family, captured the doge as he returned from mass at the church of San Pietro di Castello. He was shaved and tonsured and then forcibly ordained as a priest in Grado. Throughout its history Venice guarded against its leaders getting too self-important, and would take pains to curtail their powers appropriately.

To protect themselves against raids by the Slavs, the Venetians organized a number of expeditions; at the request of the Eastern emperor they did the same against the Saracens. For this purpose two huge ships were built, of a kind that the Greeks called *chelandrie*; they used both sails and oars and were posted to defend the two ports of the Venetian estuary. The Rivoalto islands were now becoming a city, and from a *provincia* Venice had risen to the rank of an imperial duchy, testifying to its independence from the Western Empire – although it was only a relative autonomy, since the doge, like the governments of all the other Italian communes, acknowledged the supremacy of the Empire. At this time the first coins were issued without the emperor's name and bearing the words: *Criste salva Venecias*.

The first groups of houses in what was now a major lagoon settlement had developed in rows along the *fondamente* or embankments. Many of the smaller islands were still uninhabited then, covered in dense, low vegetation that kept the wolves at bay and provided shelter for the wild birds. These early Venetian houses were one-storey affairs constructed around a court-yard. On the roof was an open veranda where clothes could be dried, and at the front, between the house and the water, was the *fondamenta*. With expanding trade in the central and northern Adriatic, the city changed. Bricks and stones slowly substituted for wood, and the attacks of the Dalmatian pirates, attracted by the city's growing wealth, made it necessary to build houses more like forts. Although no examples survive today, the fourteenth-century poet Petrarch wrote a fine description of his own house on the Riva degli Schiavoni, with its two defensive side-towers like the ones in Carpaccio's paintings.

Marshes were drained to be planted with vineyards and orchards. As more houses and *fondamente* were built, these areas gradually merged into a

single, continuous city. The canals between the rows of houses were guarded against intruders with long chains at their mouths, attached to the towers of the buildings on the outer edge of the islands. These early houses clustered around the first churches, which also served as graveyards, and grew to form the various districts of the city. The canals between these built-up areas were deepened and in some cases trees were planted along the *fondamente*, strengthening them with their roots. Wooden bridges were built over the canals, with ramps so that horses could cross them.

The geography of Venice was conditioned, then as now, by the presence of one main waterway, the Grand Canal, which snakes through the city like a reverse letter S, dividing it into two. This broad canal was probably originally the mouth of a river that flowed into the lagoon near Mestre. More than one hundred and fifty smaller canals serve as arteries of the Grand Canal Another large canal, once the mouth of the River Brenta, divides the island of Giudecca from the rest of the city.

In the ninth century, newly confirmed as a duchy, Venice was anxious

Above: *The Miracle of the Relic of the True Cross on the Rialto Bridge* by Vittore Carpaccio (1494) shows the original, wooden Rialto Bridge. In the ninth century, most Venetian houses were also made of wood.

to flaunt its increasing status. A legend asserts that the first *corno ducale* or doge's hat was donated by the Abbess of San Zaccaria, Agostina Morosini, to Doge Giovanni Partecipazio I, who had come to the abbey church to venerate the bodies of two saints donated by Pope Benedict III.

In 864 Orso Partecipazio I was elected doge and organized further military expeditions against the pirates in the Adriatic and the Saracens in southern Italy. Business as usual! But he also improved Venice itself by draining more marshes, erecting new buildings at the Rivoalto and establishing a new settlement on the island of Dorsoduro. In a solemn assembly he reaffirmed Venice's earlier ban on participating in the slave trade, which was rampant throughout the Balkans and Middle East. His prestige was so great that the Eastern Emperor conferred upon him an important title, that of *protospatharius* (meaning 'the emperor's sword-bearer' and a sign of the bond formed between Venice and the Empire), never before bestowed upon a doge. Orso responded with a gift of twelve bronze bells. He engaged personally in trade, owning four *fondachi* (trading warehouses) near Grado that were exempt from tax thanks to a treaty with the powerful patriarch of that city; the exemption did not extend to his compatriots and may have had something to do with his wife who was related to Emperor Basil.

Orso and his wife had three sons, all of whom became doges. The old Venetian legend of the *boccolo* or rosebud, which young men give girls on St Mark's Day (25 April), is attributed to a daughter of this doge, Vulcana, famous for her sparkling eyes. In love with a troubador who went to war to prove himself worthy of her, she is said to have died of a broken heart when a messenger brought her a rose that the young man had sent as a last token of his love before dying a hero's death on the battlefield.

THE DOGE'S CEREMONIAL HAT, ROBES AND REGALIA

BEFORE THE ELEVENTH CENTURY the doge's robes were sumptuously Byzantine in style, but gradually became more Italian. On their heads the earliest doges wore helmets and fur hats, or simple gold circlets that, in the thirteenth century, bore a gold decoration at the front. Beneath this, after the twelfth century, they wore a *camauro*, a bonnet of fine cloth.

The *corno ducale*, known also as a *biretum*, *corona* or *zoia*, assumed different forms over the centuries. Initially it resembled the Eastern Emperor's skullcap; it was then divided in two by a button or bow, and finally, in the thirteenth century, took the shape of the *corno* (literally 'horn'). At first sharply pointed, then more rounded, it was made of rich damask or velvet, woven with gold and silver thread and embellished with pearls and precious stones.

The ceremonial robes consisted of the *dogalina*, a kind of cassock with very broad sleeves, and a cloak with a long train and a collar of sable, ermine or wolf-skin, secured with a bejewelled gold stud. Both garments were made from the most expensive fabrics, in scarlet, purple or white. The cloak was worn on solemn feast-days, the *dogalina* alone on less important occasions. This resplendent costume was completed with hose in crimson velvet and satin, and a purple belt trimmed with silver or gold frills. The doge's signet ring bore his own image kneeling and receiving the standard from St Mark, his family coat-of-arms and the words *Voluntas ducis*.

On great occasions and in processions the doge was followed by all his insignia and badges of office, and preceded by musicians playing pipes and silver trumpets so long that boys had to hold them up, by a patrician bearing his rapier, by his personal chaplain and by the senior shield-bearer with the *corno* on a crimson velvet cushion. A gilded chair and cushion of gold cloth, surmounted by the Virgin Mary, were borne by squires, while *comandanti* followed with eight silk standards: two white for peace, two red for war, two purple for truce and two blue for union. All bore the lion of St Mark and the doge's coat-of-arms in gold.

Ceremonial was very strict, laying down exactly what the doge was to wear and when. On the Feast of the Circumcision he wore a *dogalina*, cloak and *corno* of gold and silver brocade with a sable collar, while for mourning he wore scarlet. When a doge died it was the custom for his most sumptuous clothes to be given to the churches for ecclesiastical use.

Above: The city wall ran
from the church of San
Pietro di Castello to the
centre of Venice. The
church's annual *festa*
opens the summer
season and is a lively
and popular occasion.

SYMBOLS OF STABILITY: A CITY WALL
AND A FAIRYTALE PALACE

Trade, and its uninterrupted operation, remained paramount to the rulers of
Venice. When Orso was succeeded by his son Giovanni II, one of the new
doge's first acts was to try to persuade the pope to make his brother Badoero
governor of Comacchio, a city between Venice and Ravenna; the two
territories had long been struggling for dominion over the lucrative salt trade.
For hundreds of years the control of this trade had been an important strategic
factor, and in the tenth century Venice was on the point of monopolizing it
in the Po estuary. It was salt that enabled the Venetians to procure all those
things they were unable to produce or grow themselves: in practice it was
their currency. Many areas of the lagoon were given over to salt production;
in Murano, for instance, fugitives from Altino and the mainland during the
barbarian invasions had built mills and salt-works. With the use of a kind of

dam that could be raised and lowered, salt water was let into shallow basins where it heated up and the water began to evaporate and turn into brine. It then passed through a canal into smaller basins, where it was left to evaporate again. The salt would then crystallize, after which it was ground, put into bags and stored.

While on his way to Rome, however, Badoero was attacked by the count of Comacchio, wounded in the leg and captured. He was allowed to return to Venice on condition that he would not seek recompense or revenge. But Badoero had been so badly injured that he died. To avenge him the doge attacked Comacchio, occupying and pillaging it, and devastating the surrounding lands right up to the walls of Ravenna. However, he was unable to hold the territory for long on account of opposition from the papal court.

For a warrior doge, life in these times could be brutish and short. The first action of Pietro Candiano I's dogeship in 897 was to send yet another armada against the Narentine pirates. As it did not defeat them he organized a second expedition, this time under his personal command. He was at first successful but then, in a clash near the Dalmatian coast, he and his handful of followers were killed.

Once again, Venice was threatened by invaders from the north. To protect the city against the Hungarian Tartars a huge wall was built from the Castle of Olivolo (also known as San Pietro di Castello) to Santa Maria del Giglio, where the Grand Canal was closed with a chain. This wall marked a turning-point not only in military and defensive terms, but also from a psychological point of view. In the early Middle Ages walls were symbolic as well as physical, standing for the security and stability of the city as opposed to the uncertainty of life in the countryside, forever threatened by famine and barbarian raids. At the same time communication between the lagoon islands was improved by the building of bridges and the setting up of ferry services.

In the mid-tenth century, without recourse to arms and thanks to good diplomatic relations with the Eastern Empire, Venice extended its influence into Istria, obtaining commercial tributes. The marquis of Istria resented this arrangement and began to persecute the Venetians, confiscating their goods and ships, killing their crews and obstructing their trading activities. In reprisal the Venetians set up a maritime blockade, which worked so well that the marquis begged to re-establish the old trading terms with Venice.

Two expeditions were then launched against the Croats and Slavs, including the Narentine pirates, both of which proved successful. It was during one of these engagements that, as legend recounts, the famous kidnapping of the Venetian brides took place, which developed into the tradition of the Feast of the Maries (see page 42).

ONCE VENICE'S TRADING ACTIVITIES had expanded in the Adriatic, with a continual exchange of valuable goods, such as salt, fish and wood, clashes with the Slav corsairs who operated from the delta of the River Narenta had become inevitable. The city had a dual relationship with them, as it did with the Byzantines and the Turks, based on both war and trade. The Narentines dealt in slaves, which the Venetians, for all their high-flown words, also both bought and sold. But one year during the mid-tenth century the pirates unwisely thought they would help themselves to certain Venetian commodities.

As Venice was a Christian state, marriage-bartering had been replaced by a form of public contract. Young girls would go to the church of San Pietro at the Castle of Olivolo on the Feast of the Purification of Mary to be married. The bishop would bless all the marriages on that day, in particular those of twelve poor maidens, who would be dressed in jewels and gold finery lent them by the State. The brides, in white dresses and with their hair plaited with gold thread, sat on small chests that contained their modest dowries as they awaited

THE KIDNAPPING OF THE BRIDES AND THE FEAST OF THE MARIES

their bridegrooms. After Mass and the blessing there was a feast. A ceremony very similar to this is still enacted in the mountains of Transylvania.

On this particular occasion the Narentine pirates conceived a daring plan to kidnap the brides, their dowries and the valuable ornaments. Having hidden overnight behind a sandbar, they burst in on the ceremony and carried off the terrified brides and their accoutrements. But they did not immediately set sail for the Dalmatian islands and dropped anchor to examine their booty in the lagoon of Caorle, which has ever since been called the Port of the Maidens. The outraged Venetians launched boats, followed the pirates and slaughtered the lot. The victors, captained by the doge himself, returned with the brides the same day. To commemorate the success, attributed to the intercession of the Virgin, they then instituted the week-

long Feast of the Maries, the oldest celebration in Venice.

In its original form, twelve of the most beautiful girls in Venice were adorned with splendid robes and jewels provided by rich patrician families and items from the treasury of St Mark. Services were held in the main churches and the girls travelled from one to another in processions of boats, while the city paid homage to their beauty. This attracted so many foreign visitors that the government had to take extra security measures. Wherever the Maries went, feasts were held with music and dancing, since being near the girls – or, even better, having one from one's own parish – was thought to bring good luck.

Eventually the ceremony descended into farce. The Venetians were more interested in the girls than in the religious services, so the brides were substituted by wooden puppets, which became targets for spectators throwing vegetables. This change gave rise to the term Maria di legno (wooden Mary) to indicate a cold, haughty woman; and the word 'marionette' is also said to derive from it.

The Venetians were not, however, troubled only by enemies from outside. In those years two doges from the Candiano family embarked upon a series of internecine squabbles. The son of Pietro III, Pietro IV, persuaded the people to appoint him co-regent, but this was not enough and he ended up rebelling against his father. In a tumultuous assembly convened at the Rivoalto (later abbreviated to Rialto), with many of the participants bearing arms, the supporters of the father, although he was now infirm, prevailed. The son was sent into exile. The young man and his supporters then armed a number of sailing ships in Ravenna, with which he captured various Venetian vessels. After a long struggle, in which the plague played a part, the rebellious son finally proved victorious and became doge.

One of the first acts of Pietro Candiano IV was another law to ban the slave trade and make arrangements for direct correspondence of goods between Italy and Germany and Constantinople, by means of Venetian merchants. In 962 Otto I, King of Germany, was crowned emperor in Rome by Pope John XII, inaugurating the Holy Roman Empire. But the doge no longer wished to pay allegiance to emperors of West or East and embarked on a series of self-advancing moves. He increased the family's wealth and influence by appointing his son patriarch of Grado, then repudiated his wife Giovanna, sending her off to a convent, and married the sister of the marquis of Tuscany, thus allying himself with the highest ranks of the Kingdom of Italy, with the aim of thwarting Otto. The dowry his new bride brought was a rich one, including vast estates, servants, animals, arms, ships, gold and silver, lead, zinc and iron.

In 967 the emperor himself granted the doge various privileges over the property of the Venetian clergy, and the pact with the Western Empire was renewed, with the obligation to pay a feudal tribute of 50 lire of Venetian value or 25 of imperial value. Pope John XIII recognized Grado as the patriarchate of Venice. But Venice's intimacy with the Western Empire provoked a reaction from the Eastern Empire, which used the pretext of the Venetians' illegal dealing in war contraband with the Saracens to threaten them. The doge yielded, but relations with the East did not improve.

The revived restrictions on the slave trade and on business with the Saracens, together with tax increases, aroused a great deal of discontent among the Venetians. Three of the Candiano doges had followed a policy of terrestrial expansion, with the intention of importing feudal ways of life into the city; but the people found feudalism oppressive and at odds with the city's maritime and mercantile traditions. In Germany Otto I, who had provided the doge with a force of foreign mercenaries, died, and a revolt broke out against his successor, Otto II. In 976 the Venetians followed suit, rising up against the doge. Pietro Candiano IV paid dearly for his family's tyranny and their mainland policies.

Opposite: The kidnapping of the Venetian brides by Narentine pirates.

Right: The Doge's Palace is one of Venice's most famous landmarks. It is a masterpiece of delicate design and was created as a symbol of beauty, as the city no longer had need of a fortress. The palace's close proximity to the lagoon and its apparent vulnerability emphasize the Serenissima's far-reaching political power.

IN TIME, THE CITIZENS OF VENICE came to realize how safe they were in the heart of the lagoon. In the Middle Ages, when all over Europe kings lived in heavily fortified castles, the Venetians could build a palace as an architectural flight of fancy, an intricately carved folly as graceful as a champagne glass or a piece of lace. The appearance of the palace could be regarded as a raspberry blown at Venice's enemies.

The Doge's Palace witnessed denunciations, elections, executions, intrigues and inquisitions. Containing

THE DOGE'S PALACE: AN EMBLEM OF POLITICAL POWER

all of Venice's political machinery, it was the equivalent of Downing Street, Parliament, Buckingham Palace and the Tower of London all rolled into one. The Doge's Palace was the symbol of government of the Venetian Republic, residence of the doges, seat of the highest judicial authorities and at the same time the greatest expression of Venetian Gothic architecture. A thousand years of history were played out in it: from here the Venetian aristocracy coordinated the conquest of an empire, held out against a European coalition, confronted the pope, made

war against the Turks, legislated, administered justice, survived through a combination of shrewdness and wisdom, and finally, in May 1797, abdicated.

Born as a castle in the ninth century, the palace was rebuilt and then radically reshaped in the mid-twelfth century in Veneto-Byzantine style. The present palace was built in stages over two and a half centuries; the chronicles record five destructive fires and consequent renovations, so architectural elements and decorative features from all periods now exist side by side.

The palace took on its present appearance at the end of the fifteenth century with the reconstruction of the east wing, after the two monumental façades had been built on the quay and on the Piazzetta. You enter via the *Porta del Frumento* (Door of Grain), on the quayside, which leads to an inner courtyard, a small piazza surrounded by splendid arcades. But the ceremonial entrance to the palace was via the *Porta della Carta* (Door of Paper), named either from

Opposite top: Marble carvings, like this one of Adam and Eve, adorn the façade.
Opposite below: An aerial view of the palace showing the Lido on the horizon.
Right: The Giants' Staircase, with its statues of Nepture and Mars by Sansovino.

the decrees that were hung there or because the archives were once kept nearby.

At the top of the grand *Scala dei Giganti* (Giants' Staircase) in the east wing, designed by Antonio Rizzo and dominated by Sansovino's

great statues of Mars and Neptune, each newly elected doge would swear an oath to abide by the law. On the first floor, the piano nobile, was the Doge's Apartment, looking on to the Rio di Palazzo. The Sala Grimani was used for his private audiences. Every indulgence was granted to the doge,

silver plates. The entrance wall is entirely occupied by Tintoretto's gigantic *Paradise*, while the canvases on the walls and ceiling celebrate great battles. The vestibule of the Sala del Maggior Consiglio leads to the Armoury, built as a munitions depot, and the Sala della Quarantia Civil Vecchia, who were a magistracy with jurisdiction over civil matters to do with the city and the dogeship.

The oldest façade faces the quayside, where galley captains engaged crews, paying advances on their wages. The loggia level held the rooms of the magistrates of the Piovego, which handled matters of public property; it was here that the bodies of dead doges lay in state. On the same floor were the Doge's Chancellery, the magistracy of the *Milizia da Mar* (Sea Militia), which enrolled crews for the military navy, the Avogaria, the magistracy that prepared cases to be held before the Quarantia and was in charge of registering the names of patricians in the *Libro d'Oro* (the Golden Book), and the Censors, who kept a watch on the behaviour of the patricians and tried to prevent electoral fraud.

On the upper floors were some of the most powerful organs of the State. The Signoria, the city's highest executive body, met in the Sala del Collegio, behind which was the Sala del Senato, where major policy was discussed and agreed. In one room the Quarantia Criminal met, a magistracy

with penal jurisdiction over the most serious crimes committed in the city; other rooms held the meetings of the Council of Ten who tried cases of high treason, and those of the three leaders of the Council of Ten: the supremely powerful State Inquisitors. A *bocca di leone* – a box in the shape of a lion's mouth – for secret denunciations was situated in the *Sala della Bussola* (Compass Room), while four youthful works by Hieronymus Bosch, depicting painful and grotesque scenes of torture and damnation, hung in the Saletta of the three State Inquisitors with the aim of arousing fear in those summoned to appear. An interior staircase led to the torture chamber and the Piombi, attic rooms roofed with lead (*piombo*) that were used as a prison. The Bridge of Sighs connected the palace to the main prisons – the 'sighs' were traditionally held to be those of the condemned as they crossed into incarceration.

Ambassadors saw a less dark and morbid side of the palace. They were received after climbing the glittering *Scala d'Oro* (Golden Staircase) to an endless sequence of sumptuous rooms. The most beautiful included that of the Scarlatti, where the doge's councillors would meet dressed in scarlet robes, the Sala dello Scudo, where the shield of the ruling doge was displayed, and the Sala delle Mappe, the walls of which were covered with maps of all the known world.

except that he was not allowed to speak to foreigners without supervision and every letter he wrote, even to his wife, was censored. He was allowed to receive gifts, as long as they were restricted to rose water, flowers, sweet herbs and balsam. He thus had nearly everything except his freedom, and in this way the Venetians kept their doges in check.

The Great Council met and voted in the Sala del Maggior Consiglio. In 1574 the room was prepared for a banquet in honour of Henry III of France, with three thousand guests who chose from over a thousand different dishes and three hundred varieties of sweetmeats on gold and

Previous page: The impressive Sala del Maggior Consiglio, where the Great Council met. Portraits of doges adorn the frieze.
Above: A contrast to the splendour – the torture chamber.

It was no easy matter to take the Doge's Palace, a well-defended fortress. The insurgents decided to burn it down, but the only way to do so was to set fire first to the wooden houses around it. While the fire blazed, destroying the palace, St Mark's Basilica and about three hundred houses, the doge and his son were murdered and the doge's body put on public display near the Rivoalto.

The first of two Orseolo doges was elected in the latter part of the tenth century. He rebuilt the Doge's Palace, set up a hospital for the poor near St Mark's Campanile, ordered the famous Pala d'Oro from Constantinople, then abdicated and left for a monastery in the French Pyrenees. The Pala d'Oro, a masterpiece of Byzantine and Venetian crafts-manship, is conserved behind the high altar of the Basilica. The panels depicting the story of St Mark are fused in gold compartments, and the delicacy of the enamelled figures perfectly re-creates the features of their faces, the texture of their hair and the folds of their robes. The silver frames are studded with some two thousand gems, including emeralds, sapphires, amethysts, pearls, rubies and topazes. Eight centuries later this magnificent work of art was saved from Napoleon's clutches by a courageous citizen who hid it in his own house for several months.

Towards the close of this century the dogeship of Pietro Orseolo II began with a period of uncertainty, when Otto II attempted to subjugate the Republic. He was, however, foiled by Venetian naval supremacy and then by his unexpected early death. This statesmanlike doge, so different from many of his greedy and self-seeking predecessors, proceeded to follow the kind of political guidelines that traditionally led to Venetian prosperity, as recorded in a contemporary document: 'These people do not plough, do not sow, do not harvest grapes, but draw resources of grain and wine from every port of the kingdom.' A peaceful accord was drawn up with the Western Empire, guaranteeing commercial transit on the rivers of the Po plain, which carried salt and other valuable cargoes from the estuary to other towns and cities in northern Italy for distribution throughout Europe. At the same time the doge strengthened Venetian military control over the Adriatic shipping lanes, the means of communication with the East.

Then, having rid the sea of the Slavs and placed the Dalmatian coast under his protection, he gave himself the honorific title of *Dux Dalmaticorum* (Duke of the Dalmatians). This was also the beginning of the ceremony of the mystic union of Venice with the sea.

When Pietro was succeeded by his ambitious son Otto, the Venetians did not take it well, always disliking the idea of a hereditary dogeship and recalling in particular their bad experiences with the Candiano family. Faring well at first, Otto was eventually deposed and exiled to Constantinople. From 1032, in order to prevent any future monarchical tendencies and to

RIVAL FACTIONS: THE NICOLOTTI AND THE CASTELLANI

FROM EITHER SIDE of the Grand Canal came the traditional sworn enemies known as the Castellani, named after the church of San Pietro di Castello in the eastern part of the city, and the Nicolotti, from San Nicolò dei Mendicoli in the west. The Castellani were distinguished by red caps and belts, and the Nicolotti by black. The government encouraged this conflict because it kept the population fiery-spirited and well trained in arms; also – perhaps even more usefully – it meant that if one part of the city rose up, the other would be ready to quash it: the age-old political principle of divide and rule.

The two parties would compete in the 'Labours of Hercules', which probably had their origins in the early wars of the Venetians, when, to scale the walls of cities and fortresses, the besiegers would form pyramids of men in various shapes with names such as the Lion, the Castle or the House of Mahomet. Teams of up to thirty would play this in the public squares, or on barges lashed together. Bull-chases and fist-fights were also popular, the latter taking place on a bridge known as the *Ponte dei Pugni* (the Fist Bridge). At the four corners are the marks where the combatants had to place their feet; since the bridge had no parapets, whenever people fell into the water they would be forced to separate. These fights went on until 1705 when a pitched battle broke out, starting with fists but ending with stones and knives.

Eventually the rival factions and their antics became part of Venetian pageantry, but their performances nearly always ended in tumult.

In 1810, to mark a Napoleonic anniversary, the Labours of Hercules were staged. A platform was built on boats and the audience watched from the two *fondamente*. When someone cried out that he had had his pocket picked panic broke out, aggravated by a French officer who drew his sabre and began to swish it around with the unlikely aim of restoring order. The frenzied, screaming crowd jostled together on the narrow *fondamente* and several people jumped into the boats, capsizing them.

About forty people were injured and ten killed in this incident, either drowned or crushed underfoot. In fact, the whole commotion had been started up by a Nicolotto, with the aim of distracting the Castellani players.

Opposite: The narrow streets of Castello in the eastern part of the city, where the Castellani lived. The zigzags of washing lines and the uneven paving seem to recall the local intrigues that would have taken place here.

limit the power of the dogeship, two ducal councillors were elected, one from each side of the Grand Canal. According to some accounts it marked the emergence of the two factions known as the Nicolotti and the Castellani.

Fifteen years after the Battle of Hastings when Duke William of Normandy (better known as William the Conqueror) defeated the Saxons and became king of England, the Mediterranean fell prey to the same expansionist Normans who, having seized the ports of Apulia in southeast Italy, attacked the Byzantine Empire on the eastern shores of the Adriatic. Emperor Alexius Comnenus I asked for help from the greatest power in the region, Venice. Given its vital interests in Adriatic shipping routes and in trading with Constantinople, the city was happy to oblige, and in 1081

sent a fleet to Durazzo, liberating it from a Norman siege. In return the emperor presented the doge with a gold seal, extended Venice's customs exemptions and granted official recognition to the Venetian quarter in Constantinople.

Although the Republic was not yet officially interested in involvement in crusades to the Holy Land – ostensibly to free places of Christian significance from Muslim rule – in 1099 a small private Venetian fleet set out to join the First Crusade, wintering in Rhodes en route. While it was there, ships arrived from Venice's rival Pisa – one of the four marine republics, the others being Genoa, Amalfi and Venice itself. The Venetians captured and defeated the Pisans, then set them free on condition that they would never return to Byzantine waters. The Venetian fleet, having achieved the important task of smoothing the path of their city's trade in the Eastern Mediterranean, never made it to the Holy Land. 'Venetians first, Christians afterwards' has long been our motto in Venice. The two concepts were neatly combined in their return voyage from Rhodes, when the Venetian ships escorted a group of Apulian merchants who had just stolen in Asia Minor, for their home city of Bari, the relics of St Nicholas, patron saint of sailors and the origin of Father Christmas.

SEAPOWER AND THE CONQUEST OF THE EAST

After many decades with few traces of any of my forebears, in 1122 a Giovanni da Mosto appears in a report of a session of the Nobile Consiglio. This group consisted only of noblemen, one from each *contrada* (parish), while any citizen could participate in the *Maggior Consiglio* (the Great Council). In this session Doge Domenico Michiel, successor to Ordelafo Falier who had been killed fighting the Hungarians on the Dalmatian coast, endorsed a document exempting the city of Bari in Apulia, in whose seas the Normans and Saracens rampaged freely, from customs duties.

But this was the period of the crusades, and it was the eastern end of the Mediterranean where the Saracens were most keenly opposed. Christian Europe had won the First Crusade, to the extent that Jerusalem had been taken and a Christian kingdom established. Venice, while remaining neutral, obliged private shipowners to take the crusaders to the Holy Land for immediate payment. It was only when it was realized that the rival marine republics of Pisa and Genoa were making commercial gains in the East to the detriment of Venetian interests that the city officially stepped in, equipping expeditions in support of the Kingdom of Jerusalem.

That year Doge Michiel showed his fighting spirit by taking personal command of an expedition to the Holy Land to help Baldwin II, King of Jerusalem, who was being harried by the Muslim forces. The squadron of over seventy ships arrived in the waters off Haifa when Baldwin had already been taken prisoner by the Saracens. After blockading the port and defeating the Muslim fleet the Venetians liberated the king, who in gratitude granted them the right to set up in every city of the Kingdom of Jerusalem a Venetian quarter, with its own church, square, bakery, mill, olive-press, baths, cargo wharf and system of weights and measures (with measurements such as 'feet', it was similar to the English system); Venetians were also exempted from all present and future taxes.

On his way back from the Holy Land, Michiel took Tyre, Rhodes and the city of Modone on the coast of the Morea (the modern Peloponnese) to punish the Greek Emperor John Comnenus II, who had allied himself with the Hungarians against the Republic. Then, making his way back up the Adriatic, he reconquered the Dalmatian cities that had been invaded and then devastated Belgrade (in those days Zaravecchia), which had often rebelled against Venetian rule. Emperor John II, having also lost Cephalonia, sued for peace, which was granted in 1126 in exchange for a guarantee of all previously granted privileges, confirmed by a gold seal. With the Byzantine Empire now on the verge of collapse, the Venetians promised their military support in seas freely roamed by Saracens, crusaders and Normans.

The wars for supremacy at sea and along trading routes continued incessantly in the Eastern Mediterranean, the Aegean and the Adriatic, on whose coasts the Norman ruler Roger II, King of the Two Sicilies, continued his expansionist policy. It was in these years that two enormous columns of pink and grey granite were brought to Venice from the East and later erected in the Piazzetta near St Mark's, where they stand as symbols of Venetian history.

According to the sculptor and architect Jacopo Sansovino, there were originally three columns, but as they were being unloaded one fell into the water and could not be retrieved. As for the other two, it was not until many years later that Nicolò Barattieri, the master craftsman from Lombardy, ingeniously succeeded in raising them. He tied each one tightly with thick ropes soaked in water; as the ropes dried they grew taut, pulling the column up a little; sandbags were immediately squeezed in beneath the column to hold it in place, and in this way, the ropes being alternately soaked and dried, each column was slowly brought upright. On top were placed the symbols of Venice: St Theodore, first protector of Venice, with his curious dragon-crocodile emblem, and the winged lion, derived from ancient Sassanian or Chinese art, which represented St Mark. Barattieri's enterprise was so highly appreciated by the Senate that he was given permission to set up a gaming-table on the steps of the columns, which made him enormously rich.

THE SIX *SESTIERI* AND THEIR ORIGINS

———

SINCE THE EARLY MIDDLE AGES the districts of Venice have consisted of six *sestieri* (districts). Three of them, Castello, San Marco and Cannaregio, lie on one side of the Grand Canal, while on the other are San Polo, Santa Croce and Dorsoduro, the last of which used to include Giudecca and the island of San Giorgio Maggiore (now a separate district). This division seems to have originated with the election of six counsellors of the Serenissima Signoria, one for each *sestiere*.

Castello, the easternmost *sestiere* and one of the larger islands on which Venice was founded, was originally called Olivolo. The later name is said to come either from the ruins of a castle that the Roman historian Livy mentions as having been constructed by Antenor, leader of the Heneti, at the northern end of the Adriatic, or

known as *Canna recium* from its numerous marshy reedbeds. There used to be windmills in this district. San Marco is self-explanatory, although in ancient times this area was known as *Morso* (bite) because its soil was more resistant than elsewhere, and *Brolo* (orchard) because it was grassy and surrounded by trees.

On the other side of the Grand Canal, the church of Santa Croce is said to have been founded by settlers fleeing from the Lombard invasion. Some authorities, however, believe that the wealthy Badoer family gave the land to the Benedictines for a monastery, but the monks' licentious behaviour caused them to be thrown out in the mid-fourteenth century.

Dorsoduro is a group of islets between the Grand Canal and the Giudecca Canal. The name (literally 'hard back') may refer to its hard soil, but some documents refer to it as Dossoduro, from the Dosduri family, one of the first to flee here from Padua. In the early days the area was sparsely inhabited because it was relatively exposed to barbarian raids;

yet some claim that, as the area lay 'beyond the tower' of Castel Forte at San Rocco, it took its name from the Latin *deorsum turris*.

In the ninth century two Tradonico doges founded the first church of St Paul or, in Venetian dialect, San Polo, which gave its name to the *sestiere* where I was born and still live. On the campanile erected in 1362 can be seen two lions, one of which has a snake curled around its neck, while the other holds a severed human head between its paws – possibly an allusion to a *condottiere* (mercenary leader) who was beheaded for treachery against the Republic. In the mid-fourteenth century, on St Paul's Day, a great earthquake struck Venice; the Grand Canal was drained and a thousand houses collapsed. After this catastrophe the custom arose of referring to the poor saint as 'St Paul of the earthquake'.

Left and above: Dorsoduro, one of Venice's six *sestieri*, is a district of small meandering canals and scented walled gardens.

from a castle that was built on Olivolo to defend the Rivoalto isles, guarding the port of San Nicolò.

The name Cannaregio may derive from the Canal Regio or Regal Canal that cuts north through this *sestiere* from the Grand Canal to the lagoon. Others claim that the area was once

Above: St Mark's Basin with the distinctive island of San Giorgio Maggiore in the background. The two granite columns brought from the East can be seen next to the Doge's Palace. Even today, with the age of public executions long gone, Venetians consider it bad luck to walk between the columns.

Later, criminals were executed or punished between the two columns. A contemporary account gives an impression of curiosity rather than revulsion: 'This morning … in the piazza I saw the spectacle of two drowned men, three in the stocks and two hanged.' Even today, Venetians consider it bad luck to pass between the columns.

A certain Vito da Mosto nearly had closer acquaintance with these two columns than he would have wished. In 1524 he and some accomplices were arrested for forging coins, and duly tortured and imprisoned – the chronicles of the time reveal that it was permitted to forge only foreign coins. Vito and his patrician friend Natale Contarini were exiled to Cyprus and warned that if either of them returned to Venice he would be taken between the two columns to have one of his eyes put out. Fortunately Vito reformed and I discovered him, ten years later, responsible for collecting State taxes on *panni d'oro* (golden fabrics) and later employed directly by the Venetian mint. He certainly had the right professional background.

The city had now consolidated itself so that all political and administrative matters were dealt with in the area between St Mark's and the Rivoalto. The islands and more distant parts of the lagoon continued to live by fishing, hunting and farming. It was at about this time that the city began to be divided into districts known as *sestieri*, each under its own ducal councillor. But although the seat of power on land may have been small, Venice was now virtually the uncontested ruler of the seas. The city's naval superiority was based on the great stout-walled Arsenale – the very heart of Venice's seapower, as it was defined by the Senate in an early sixteenth-century document. The Venetian Arsenale – a word assimilated into many other languages to indicate primarily a munitions store – was a naval base, a place for ship maintenance and outfitting, a depot for equipment, provisions and weapons, and an active ship-building yard. Security was extremely tight.

Founded by Doge Ordelafo Falier in 1104, it became the heart of Venice's sea prowess. It was first enlarged to four times its original size in the fourteenth century, when Dante described it in his *Inferno* as the place where the 'tenacious pitch boils in the winter'. By the sixteenth century this great naval installation, the largest productive complex and the greatest concentration of skilled labour in the world prior to the industrial age, had attained its present dimensions and employed more than fifteen thousand carpenters alone.

In 1570, when the Turks attacked Cyprus, the Arsenale had furnished a hundred galleys ready for combat within just two months, in part building them, in part adapting the commercial fleet. A century earlier the production-line system had been invented at the Arsenale and, for the benefit of King

Below: The extensive ship yards of the Arsenale, the heart of Venice's sea power for hundreds of years – a city within a city.

Henry III of France, an entire galley was assembled during a banquet. Organization and subdivision of labour, quality control and standardization of most of the production processes at the Arsenale all anticipated the criteria of modern factories.

Close by on the Riva degli Schiavoni were the cereal storehouse and the bakeries, where the famous biscuit-bread was made for the Republic's ships as well as for garrisons overseas. Many streets in the district of Castello, where the Arsenale is situated, are named after its activities: *Calle della Pece* (pitch), *del Piombo* (lead), *delle Ancore* (anchors), *degli Scudi* (shields) and *delle Vele* (sails).

This great enterprise was administered by a council consisting of three senators and three 'patrons', all members of the Great Council. The aristocracy had a clear sense of its responsibilities and duties – the patrons took it in turns to sleep in the Arsenale in order to guard the keys to the warehouses and workshops and to inspect the night watchmen.

On the technical side the Arsenale was under the charge of the Magnificent Admiral, who controlled the complex and wide-ranging activities of carpenters, caulkers, oarmakers, smiths, sawyers and powder-magazine men working with hemp, pitch, ropes, gunpowder and other materials, but especially wood.

The Venetian Republic was founded on wood: vast numbers of poles thrust into the mud enabled its palaces to stand, and timber kept its ships ploughing through the seas. The head carpenter from the Arsenale would go into the State-owned forests to choose oaks, larches or beeches that were best suited in shape and quality to the various parts of the ships; in many cases the branches were trained to curve as they grew. One of the basins of the Arsenale was given over to the conservation and seasoning of timber; once soaked in salt water, the wood became resistant to it, as well as immune to woodworm and other harmful parasites.

After the wood was seasoned the sawyers cut the trunks, following the grain, to obtain the planking. Then the *marangoni* (carpenters) fashioned the elements that were to form the keel and ribbing. The oarmakers had the task of shaping a long pole of beechwood into an oar that would be strong, light and perfectly balanced, between 7 and 9 metres (23 and 29½ feet) long according to the position of the oarsman on the benches.

The construction slips occupied almost all the docksides; elsewhere were the *velene*, where the sails were cut and sewn; the *corderia* (rope factory), almost 300 metres (984 feet) long, where a great stone face with a gigantic mouth paid out the heavy rope; and a foundry for producing metal items, such as nails and crossbows.

Because of the responsibility and the skill and precision required for their jobs, the *arsenalotti* enjoyed high wages and numerous privileges, but

Opposite: A corner of the Arsenale from Rio della Tana (which refers to the area where hemp for the ships' ropes was grown). The *arsenalotti*, who were highly skilled and well provided for by the Serenissima, lived close by.

no mistakes were permitted. They were known as the 'Republic's favourite children'. Once their names had been enrolled in the Arsenale paybook, they had a job for life and were paid even when old or sick. The Republic encouraged the *arsenalotti* to hand on their skills and crafts to their children, and for this purpose maintained a school inside the Arsenale.

These highly skilled and experienced craftsmen worked in buildings designed by the best architects of the times. The *Tana* or *Casa del Canevo* (House of Hemp) appears in the reconstruction of 1579–83 by Antonio da Ponte, who also designed the Rialto Bridge and the palazzo where I live. Michele Sanmicheli built the slip for the *Bucintoro* in the 1540s, and Jacopo Sansovino designed the functional and elegant watersheds known as the Gaggiandre in the same period. The artillery store was described by some of the illustrious visitors allowed in for propaganda purposes as a 'garden of iron'; on the fall of the Republic in 1797 more than five thousand guns were found there, all subsequently looted by Napoleon to be melted down.

Skilled oarsmen and state-of-the-art ships were certainly in demand at this time, for the commercial supremacy of Venice and the other maritime republics had begun to cause resentment among the Byzantine Greeks. The situation degenerated when Emperor Manuel Comnenus destroyed the Genoese quarter in Constantinople and dispersed the Venetian colony,

arresting the residents and confiscating their estates. In 1171 Doge Vitale Michiel II led a squadron into the Aegean, but returned with his crews decimated by plague and without having achieved anything.

Back in Venice after this setback, he reformed the system for electing the doge by members of the *Maggior Consiglio* (Great Council). In the mid-twelfth century a new body was instituted 'for the honour, benefit and safety of this our country' – the *Consilium Sapentium* (Council of the Wise), with some thirty-five members. This council, presided over by the doge, was the nucleus of the subsequent Great Council. Although restricted by Vitale Michiel II to four hundred and eighty members, chosen from among the leading families and elected anually, over the years its membership increased to more than a thousand. The numbers rose whenever the coffers of the Republic had to be lined for wars against its traditional enemies, the Genoese and the Turks. Middle-class families that had been citizens for over four hundred years were granted, for an appropriately large fee, an entry in the Golden Book of the nobility.

Whether they wanted to or not, my da Mosto ancestors always participated in the great assemblies. On occasion, by disagreeing with the authorities and perhaps insulting the doge or other councillors, they got themselves exiled.

The Great Council elected the doge by a system that grew ever more complex and intricate, so anxious were the Venetians to prevent it becoming a hereditary office and to pre-empt electoral fraud. In the Room of the Great Council in the Doge's Palace stood an urn containing a sphere for each member; thirty were gold and the rest silver. Each councillor drew out a sphere; the thirty who found gold chose nine from among themselves; these nine then elected another forty, who then chose twelve from among themselves; these in turn elected another twenty-five, who chose another nine from among themselves, who elected another forty-five who chose eleven from among themselves, who elected the forty-one councillors who would at last elect the doge. At the end of this tortuous process the final forty-one assembled, amid strict security similar to that still enforced today for the election of popes, and, following rigid rules, the candidate with most preferences above a minimum of twenty-five became doge.

The common people were therefore now excluded from the election of the doge, who would henceforth merely be presented to them with the words: 'Here is your doge, if it pleases you.' It did *not*, of course, please the people, who some years later rose up and assassinated Vitale Michiel II. His successor Sebastiano Ziani, instituted the prudent ritual of scattering largesse to the people on election day. He was also responsible for a number of public works in the city, including the first wooden bridge over the Grand Canal at the Rialto. It was first planned in 1178 by Nicolò Barattieri – built on boats and movable pontoons, lashed together, it was known as the Ponte dei Due Soldi, as it replaced the *due soldi* (two coins) ferry service.

Meanwhile, the current Holy Roman emperor, Frederick Barbarossa – so called because of his long red beard – had been casting covetous eyes on Italy. He was fiercely opposed by the pope and by the Lombard League, an alliance of northern Italian cities that included Venice. Barbarossa was eventually defeated at the Battle of Legnano, and the Venetians achieved a major diplomatic coup when a peace agreement was signed in 1177 in St Mark's Basilica by the emperor and Pope Alexander III. This peace treaty confirmed Venice's independence from other Italian cities and increased the prestige of the Republic throughout Europe. But there were some uneasy moments before the two great men committed themselves. It is said that when the emperor entered St Mark's and prostrated himself, as was the custom, before the pope the latter, instead of bidding him to rise, placed his foot on the imperial neck and quoted from the Bible: 'You will walk on the viper and trample on the lion and dragon.' When Frederick replied: 'I pay homage not to you, but to Peter', Alexander's icy rejoinder was: 'To St Peter *and* to me.'

It may have been on this occasion that Alexander III donated the ring used in the ceremony later known as the *Sposalizio del Mare* (Marriage with

ENRICO DANDOLO AND THE QUARREL WITH THE GREEKS

————

THE EMPEROR IN CONSTANTINOPLE in the late twelfth century was Manuel Comnenus, attractive, devious, urbane and decadent: Manuel's conquests even included his own niece. But beyond the bedroom he sought to rebuild the power and the glory of his empire and in particular to re-establish Byzantine control over Italy – in other words, to reclaim overall supremacy in the Eastern Mediterranean. Venice, of course, was a thorn in his side.

As the influence of Venice spread, its merchants and traders had created a huge enclave in Constantinople. Then, suddenly, they were *persone non gratae*: in just a few days thousands of them were stripped of their possessions and entire families were thrown into jail. The Venetian government sent two delegations,

which Manuel completely ignored. Then, in March 1172, the patrician and future doge Enrico Dandolo was sent as ambassador in a final attempt at reconciliation.

History records that this great Venetian received the usual treatment – ignored at first, then humiliated. One legend suggests that he was beaten up and had his skull fractured, another that after an angry confrontation Manuel ordered him to be blinded. At any rate, when Dandolo returned home later that year he is said to have been blind. But was he? In Venice no one was allowed to sign a legal document unless they could read it themselves, and Enrico Dandolo's signature appears on legal documents dated four years later.

He himself remained vague about the exact details of his blindness, saying it was the result of a blow to the head. Was he too humiliated to tell the truth? Or was it simply useful propaganda to stir up his fellow

citizens? The story of Dandolo's blinding in Constantinople had spread like wildfire and only added to their outrage, although the Venetians scarcely needed an excuse to direct their anger against the Byzantines. Blind or not, and a virtual recluse in his palace on the Rialto, he did not abandon the cause of the Republic and was constantly sought out for advice on public matters.

In 1193 Enrico Dandolo was elected doge and greeted with acclaim; the Venetians had found a master tactician, brilliant strategist and consummate politician, a leader whose aspirations were as ruthlessly ambitious as their own. He was, in short, a liar, a cheat, a master of deceit, skulduggery, double dealing and political spin – ideal qualifications for a patriotic doge whose determined aim was to strengthen the Venetian Republic and its trading prospects. The Fourth Crusade, to retake Constantinople, was his masterstroke.

the Sea). However, the ceremony had already been in existence for some time and other legends exist – for instance, that the doge had received the ring from a fisherman who had been given it by St Mark in person. For this showy spectacle, in which the Adriatic was named 'Gulf of Venice' on account of the city's victories over the Dalmatian pirates, the doge, dressed in gold and ermine and with the *corno* on his head, would sail in the *Bucintoro*, the elaborately carved and gilded galley of the doges, to the harbour mouth of San Nicolò on the Lido, where the patriarch awaited him. Here the doge would throw the wedding ring into the waters and pronounce the ritual

words: 'We marry you, O sea, in a sign of true and perpetual dominion, asking God to protect those who travel by sea.' It is said that in later years, to economize, the ring was only symbolically thrown into the Adriatic after the patriarch had blessed it, and that a bucket of holy water was poured into the sea instead.

The stage was now set for one of the great moments of Venetian history, a perfect example of the way the Republic was able to aggrandize itself by way of clever commercial and diplomatic dealings. The event on which it all hinged was the Fourth Crusade, and after it Venice would be more glorious, and more powerful, than ever before.

In 1187 the Christian troops of the Kingdom of Jerusalem, under attack by the ferocious Saladin, Sultan of Egypt, had been unable to defend their city, despite European aid, and it had fallen into Muslim hands. And so a new crusade was organized by Count Baldwin of Flanders, and Venice – in particular the Venetian fleet – was officially asked to participate. The stated destination of this expedition was Egypt, regarded as the soft underbelly of the Islamic world. Through military action the Republic had now proved itself to be the strongest power in the Eastern Mediterranean, able to rely upon a well-distributed series of secure trading bases.

In 1203 Doge Enrico Dandolo, eighty years old and almost blind but a skilful leader and intuitive strategist, contracted to transport twenty thousand crusaders to Egypt in ships stocked with a year's provisions, and to provide another fifty armed vessels to protect the convoy. The crusaders guaranteed to pay the Venetians an enormous sum and to grant them half the war booty. But things did not go as planned: there were few soldiers and no money. And so – perhaps having had this idea in the back of their minds all along – the Venetians did a deal.

Relations between Venice and Constantinople had been strained for a long time. The Greeks resented the Venetians' commercial success, while the Venetians in turn objected to the high-handed way their citizens were treated within the Byzantine Empire. It was an opportunity for the doge to settle some scores. He urged the crusaders' leaders to divert to Constantinople (subduing en route, on Venice's behalf, a difficult neighbour on the Dalmatian coast); then, having taken the Byzantine capital, they would replace the present half-mad emperor with a younger, more compliant candidate.

At first the crusaders attacked Constantinople from the land, but were driven back; then the Venetians, directed by old Dandolo himself, assaulted the great walls from the ships that had entered the Golden Horn and took the city. But the succession did not go as planned; another contender for the throne presented himself, and mob violence broke out. Faced with a dangerous uprising, in 1204 the crusaders decided to conquer Constantinople a second time. After a sturdy defence by the Greeks, this sumptuous city

Opposite: A model of the *Bucintoro*, the richly decorated galley of the doges that was used for the traditional 'Marriage of the Sea' ceremony.

THE MERCHANT PALACES
_____

THE PALACES ALONG THE GRAND CANAL embody, in both structure and style, not only the history of Venetian architecture but also the entrepreneurial nature of the city's ruling class. One of the most ancient surviving examples is the Ca' da Mosto, where my family once lived. Originally a two-storey building in Veneto-Byzantine style, erected in the thirteenth century, it was decorated with sculptures taken from ninth-century Byzantine buildings and still shows traces of being a *casa-fondaco*, both home and workplace of the merchant owner. Such houses have two entrances, one on the water and the other from the land.

The distribution of the arches and the windows on different levels of the façade reflects the function of the *casa-fondaco* and the hierarchy of its internal spaces. The typical layout consisted of a central core with an arcade and loggia flanked by two small side-towers, echoing late Roman architecture but with a fusion of Eastern and Western features that

is characteristic of Venice. The Ca' da Mosto retains this basic shape, with a large longitudinal room in the centre; on the *piano nobile*, the first floor, this is marked by the multi-arched window in the façade, flanked by two rows of rooms.

The great room on the ground floor of a *casa-fondaco*, with its canal entrance and courtyard access, served primarily for the loading and unloading of goods and only secondarily as a monumental entrance hall; the side rooms were used for storage. The external staircase led to the first-floor *salone*. The two wings on either side of this entrance hall were divided vertically to create an *ammezzato* (half-storey), where the merchant's *mezà* (administrative offices) were situated. On the *piano nobile* the *portego* (the great central room) was the place where samples of merchandise would be displayed to

clients; later it became a splendid setting for parties and receptions. Further up, the storey directly beneath the roof was where dependants and servants lived.

Palaces, especially from the Renaissance onwards, became the increasingly sumptuous homes of wealthy patricians. They still never lost their basic structural features, even though they underwent major decorative changes whenever new artistic influences reached the lagoon. Most of the palaces on the Grand Canal were built in the last four centuries of the Republic, long after the days of those early merchants and entrepreneurs who created the city's fortunes and conceived the *casa-fondaco*; however, they remained faithful to the spirit of Venetian architecture, a vibrant harmony of stone, water, light and air. The Byzantine style of the East combined with the Gothic style of Western Europe, created a bizarre, unique fusion. No other city in the world looked, or looks, like this.

was taken and stripped of its treasures in three days of pillaging and destruction. Venice's portion, carefully selected for its prestige value, included the enamels and precious oriental marble-work used for the Pala d'Oro and the four bronze horses of St Mark's Basilica. Soon to become the crowning glory of the world's most extraordinary trophy cabinet, six centuries later they were irresistible to another souvenir-hunter, Napoleon, who bore them off to Paris.

The Latin Empire of the East was now set up under a new emperor, Count Baldwin of Flanders. In the share-out of Byzantine lands, Venice took possession of a good portion of Constantinople as well as territory extending from Dalmatia to the Aegean, Cyprus and the Black Sea, with strategic bridgeheads that included the island of Candia (Crete) – in times to come, a perpetual battlefield for the Venetians. With these acquisitions, the doge became 'Lord of a Quarter and a Half-quarter of the Roman Empire'.

Some of the aristocratic merchant families, such as the Contarini and the Querini, now set up their own small fleets of trading ships; one of the Querini galleys was under the command of a certain Girolamo da Mosto from my own branch of the family tree.

Those who think of the nobleman of those times as someone who wielded power from a castle and had feudal rights over land and its occupants may be puzzled by the figure of the Venetian patrician, who was simply a merchant devoted to navigation and commerce. However, nobility, in the sense of the quality of the ruling class, can be acquired and exercised in many different ways. Private and public achievement was a main characteristic of the Venetian aristocracy; a sense of enterprise, tempered by hard experience, made the Venetian nobleman a strong personality, able to serve both his family and the Republic.

For example, the proceedings of the Great Council report that in 1412 Daniele Renier justified the absence of his twenty-year-old son by explaining that he was embarked on the galleys to Alexandria; the father participated in political life while the son worked on board ship. It was a realistic approach to life. The noblemen were always ready to play their roles, whether it was a matter of commanding galleys or negotiating with kings; they knew that their reputations had to be earned every day by hard sacrifice, and they were conscious not only of their rights but of their duties towards the city. Every patrician was convinced not that he was serving the Republic, but that he was himself a part of the Republic. When two of them were invited to the coronation of a king of England, who wished to bestow an honorific title on them, they refused because the ceremony would oblige them to kneel before the monarch. This, they explained, was impossible for a patrician citizen of the Republic.

The boyhood of a nobleman was devoted to study, though on a practical

Page 68: The beautiful Gothic tracery on the Ca' d'Oro shows another aspect of Venetian architecture. Amazingly the façade used to be covered in gold leaf. Previous page: The Ca' da Mosto, the home of my ancestors, is one of the oldest surviving Byzantine palaces.

level: he had to be able to read and write and do accounts to enable him to engage in commerce. In his father's house the lad would already be in contact with ships, merchandise and sailors from overseas. When he was a little older, he became a crossbowman: every shipowner was obliged to take on, as paid armed escorts, a number of young patricians, who could also engage in a little trade. This was a highly formative apprenticeship. The young man had to learn self-reliance, and get used to the difficulties of shipboard life, to discipline, to the dangers of navigation and to the crafty ways of Easterners. He also learned the arts of sailing and commerce, as well as foreign languages, and became acquainted with different lands and peoples.

Since the sea lanes were infested with both pirates and Turks, there was little difference between a navigator and a warrior: anyone who signed on had to be prepared to fight. There was no shortage of advice from relatives. Benedetto Sanudo told his younger brother, embarking for the first time: 'Obey the commander, don't play cards on board, take a few books because the voyage is long, don't eat exotic foods, avoid the loose women of Crete and keep well wrapped up.'

They left the comforts of home at all ages. A member of the Canal family commanded a galley at the age of twenty-two, and took his four-year-old son with him, feeding the boy hard tack; Francesco Balbi continued to trade until he was eighty-four. While Benedetto Barbaro travelled through Syria collecting ancient medals, Marco Bollani drowned when his wrecked galley was dragged down by the five kilos of gold he had refused to relinquish. Thirteen young noblemen organized a theatre company in Constantinople. Antonio Paruta summoned his nephew to that city to learn Turkish, while Giovanni Contarini studied at the Sorbonne and at Oxford and at the same time continued to sell spices for his family business.

Subsequently the notion of merchant, covering ship-owning, managerial and organizational activities, fell into disuse in Venice. While life for the patrician of the early days was arduous but adventurous, in the opulent society of Venice's golden age luxury and display became the rule. So the patrician, thanks to opportunities and place of residence, found himself at the centre of a world whose priorities were cultural; pleasure and ostentation took precedence over everything, and their brilliant world proved too fragile to withstand the harsh winds of political change from without.

But back in the thirteenth century, with the Byzantine Empire and its aspirations now consigned to history, the Venetian Republic reigned supreme as a mercantile state. The years of its monopoly over the great trading routes between East and West, which radiated from the Rialto throughout Europe, were just beginning. The *Stato da Mar* – the sea-based colonial empire, as opposed to the *Stato da Terra* or land-based possessions – had come to life.

Overleaf: Some of the grand palaces are now grand hotels. This is the Bauer Grunwald on the Grand Canal. Other palaces have now become offices.

2

EARTH

THE BOUNDARIES OF LAND ENLARGE

The taking of Constantinople and the subsequent share-out of the strategically useful parts of the Byzantine 'Empire' represented a triumphant moment for Venice, a significant asset for the *Stato da Mar*. This success aroused the hostility of other great seapowers, in particular arch-rival Genoa, as well as the Greek-Byzantines themselves, who sought revenge. These two powers formed an alliance: in exchange for help in reconquering Byzantium, the Greeks would grant Genoa all the privileges currently held by Venice.

Venice won the first round in 1257 at St John of Acre in Syria. The Venetian commercial fleet of the East, and a war squadron led by the doge's son, Lorenzo Tiepolo, broke the chain that barred the port and set fire to the Genoese ships. The Venetians returned home, as ever, with booty: the two great pillars of Acre, which now stand in front of the Porta della Carta of the Doge's Palace.

The success in Syria was not the end of things: Constantinople was soon reoccupied by the Greek-Genoese coalition under the leadership of Michael Paleologus, thereby ending the Latin Empire of the East. Through negotiation with Paleologus, however, the Venetians managed to keep their territories in Crete and the Morea as a defence against the Genoese, whose aggressiveness was forcing the Republic to adopt an expensive system of escorted convoys. Eventually war fever gave way to diplomacy on other matters, too. Despite Venice still being at war with his allies the Genoese, Paleologus readmitted the Venetians' commercial interests to Constantinople. In 1270 a peace settlement was reached, the Genoese being forced into compliance by Louis IX of France.

Opposite: Outside the Scuola di San Rocco. Venice is often referred to as a large *salotto* (sitting room), or as a living theatre, with its splendid monumental backdrop.

It was with the election of Lorenzo Tiepolo as doge in 1268 that the complex, multi-stage electoral system (see page 64) was introduced; it endured, with some slight modifications, until the end of the Republic. After centuries of violent internecine warfare, in which doges were deposed, jailed, blinded or assassinated and power was restricted to a few families, the city gradually created institutions that could guarantee a fairer and more stable form of government, impose obedience at home, make itself respected abroad, provide firm leadership and concern itself with public welfare. The government was not at the service of any party and could therefore aim to be both impartial and firm. The Venetians depicted their city as the figure of Justice, using her scales and sword to apply the rules serenely (see page 66). Hence 'Serenissima', the Most Serene Republic, a sobriquet applied to Venice from the Middle Ages. The mythical figure of the woman with the scales provided an ideal for the Venetian governing class to strive to meet.

Although the historic social divisions remained, everyone in the Republic was equal insofar as all were expected to serve their country. In a later document, the mid-sixteenth-century *De Magistratibus et Republica Venetorum*, Gasparo Contarini, a Venetian politician, diplomat and cardinal, summed up the secret of Venice's success as its system of government, which contained the three forms theorized by Aristotle: monarchy (with the doge), oligarchy or government of the few (with the Senate and the Council of Ten), and democracy or government of the many (with the Great Council).

By the mid-twelfth century the doge was already assisted at decisive moments by the *Consiglio dei Savi* (Council of the Wise), appointed by the popular assembly. Later it was established that twelve electors, two from each of the six *sestieri*, should each elect forty citizens who would form the 480-strong Great Council, which had replaced the old popular assembly. Alongside this was the so-called Lesser Council of six members, one from each *sestiere*. Slowly the Great Council, later backed up by an ever more powerful Council of Ten, became the real government of the Venetian State, while the doge, with the Lesser Council and the leaders of the Quarantia, which had judicial powers, represented the executive authority or the Signoria. Subsequently numerous bodies were created to back up the Great Council. These Collegi dei Savi, or Committees of the Wise, had jurisdiction over areas such as nautical matters, internal affairs, managing lagoon resources, war and finance.

The doge was the highest authority in the State and he was elected for life, but was wisely limited by a system of checks and balances so that the role gradually became more a representative than an effective one; he served to symbolize the aristocracy. The Senate was actually the most important institution of the Republic, but its actions were in any case

Opposite: The courtyard of the Doge's Palace enclosed on all sides by porticos and containing two enormous bronze well-heads. Now mainly a museum, one wing also contains offices of the executive agency of the Ministry for Culture and Architectural Heritage, which oversees projects for the conservation, preservation and restoration of Venice.

subject to the control of the Council of Ten. It was said that the councillors could not do much without the doge, but that the doge could do nothing without them.

The aristocracy had a clear sense of its responsibilities and duties: anyone who blotted his reputation was permanently excluded from the patriciate. Anyone who refused a position to which he had been appointed or who performed it inadequately lost his political rights, and anyone who married outside his social class was alienated.

Medieval Venice, capital of a state that was already rich and powerful, was socially and politically advanced in many ways. Its constitution forbade any intermingling of Church and State; ecclesiastics could not share in the work of the Great Council, even if they were noblemen. Although unable to take part in the election of the doge from the end of the fourteenth century, the middle classes and the ordinary people were not excluded from political life altogether – indeed, many important posts in administration, the army and the navy were specifically reserved for them. Moreover, the rich and powerful trade associations could discuss their particular needs with the government, and were able to influence the city's domestic and foreign policies.

Legislation was enacted to cover all areas in political and civic life, such as the management of the lagoon. The river estuaries that impacted on the navigability of its waters were kept under constant observation and, when necessary, their courses were diverted to prevent them silting up. The government was prepared to go to war, if need be, to ensure its freedom to carry out essential hydraulic works or to stop activities that it considered harmful.

The pioneering nature of the medieval Venetian Republic is symbolized by a contemporary law to control under-age labour; no such legislation was enacted anywhere else in Europe until Britain did so five centuries later. A mid-thirteenth-century statute forbade doctors to have any interests in common with pharmacists and to prolong treatment unnecessarily in order to increase their profits; from the early fourteenth century the Republic itself had a number of doctors on its payroll, thus instituting an early form of public-health service.

But advances in social welfare could do little in the face of acts of God: at around the same time there was a major earthquake in Venice, causing great destruction and loss of life. Assaults were meanwhile made on lesser trading rivals, such as the port of Ancona, and tariff wars were waged against Bologna. This was also the period in which the Venetian mint began the production of the famous gold ducat, soon to become currency way beyond the Republic, reflecting Venice's strength as a far-reaching, trading nation.

Above: Part of my family's collection of Venetian coins – *grossi*, *zecchini* and *oselle* – with examples from Doge Dandolo's rule in the twelfth century to that of Doge Mocenigo IV in the eighteenth century, produced just twenty-nine years before the end of the Republic.
Opposite: The *Zecca* (mint) designed by Sansovino played a vital part in Venice's history by devising innovative financial instruments.

A FINANCIAL POWERHOUSE

THE FIRST VENETIAN MINT was set up in the ninth century, and to begin with the city used either its own silver coins or gold ones minted in Byzantium. In 1284 it began to coin the gold ducat, later known as the *zecchino*, from an Arabic word for the right to be named on coins – the modern word 'sequin' derives from it. The ducat remained the principal measure of wealth throughout the late Middle Ages and after, and was a readily acceptable currency throughout Europe, Africa and Asia because of the Republic's great wealth and stability. Its fine gold content, about 3½ grams, corresponded to the price of an item of clothing, a good dinner with friends or the services of a lady of easy virtue but only average beauty.

Venice also invented the concept of the public debt. All medieval governments financed their wars by short-term loans that paid interest at between 12 and 20 per cent, but Venice was the first European state to consolidate these loans as the public debt – loans to the State – in what was known as the *Monte Vecchio* (Old Mountain). The Republic made extensive use of the public debt to finance itself and managed, right to the end of its days and despite wars and other setbacks, to maintain a favourable ratio between the sum of its revenues and the payments made to lenders. When the French ambassador Philippe de Commines wrote at the end of the fifteenth century that Venice was the 'most wisely' governed city, one of the reasons was undoubtedly the shrewdness with which the Venetian governing class handled financial matters. Indirect taxation, the equivalent of Britain's value added tax and customs duties, was for a long time preferred to direct taxation, such as income tax.

Around the year 1500 Venice was the greatest maritime power in the Mediterranean and the greatest Italian state. Outlays and incomes from its overseas possessions were well balanced; incomes from the mainland cities, on the other hand, were far superior to outlays. The incomes now included direct taxes, instituted to substitute the system of loans to pay for wars. A compulsory loan was no better to the provider than direct taxation, particularly if the interest rates were cut. Finally, as an example of Venetian financial acumen, it is worth noting that the city always had capital available for special projects. This helps to explain why neither the League of Cambrai nor the Turks, both powerful adversaries, managed to undermine Venice's real strength.

A few years earlier, while relations were still peaceful with the Bolognese, a certain Marco da Mosto and his fellow merchant Giacomo Donà had bought from them a cargo of salts of Cervia, a substance whose value was constantly fluctuating. It seems, sadly, that they lost the trade window and therefore their money. A more important event in the history of Venetian commerce was the departure of two merchants, the brothers Nicolò and Matteo Polo, for Asia (see opposite).

The final years of the thirteenth century were a dark period for the Republic, marked by great changes, few of them desirable, both at home and abroad. In addition to earthquakes and floods, a papal interdict was proclaimed by Pope Martin IV in response to Venice's failure to participate in a crusade he had launched against an unacceptable regime in Sicily, sparked off by a massacre known as the Sicilian Vespers. Other challenges included a further crusade against the Saracens and wars with the Eastern Emperor, in which the Venetians managed to defeat his Genoese allies in the Black Sea.

Rivalry between the two marine republics over trade in that region continued unabated. The Genoese preferred large-scale naval battles, opting for the immediate trophies of war booty, whereas the Venetians were more strategic in the way they conducted hostilities. After a series of skirmishes, the great naval battle of Curzola was fought in 1298. The Venetians had the worse of it, but the Genoese suffered such heavy losses that they were unable to pursue their enemy into the lagoon. The eventual settlement formalized Genoa's primacy over the Ligurian coast and Venice's over the Adriatic. But the antagonism between the two in the East was still simmering beneath the surface.

The previous year had seen a major administrative upheaval known as the *Serrata del Maggior Consiglio* (Locking of the Great Council), which marked the official birth of the Venetian patriciate. Admission to the Great Council would now be granted only to those who currently belonged to it or had done so during the previous four years, subject to the approval of the Quarantia. New candidates also had to receive the approval of the Quarantia. Later the rules for admission were made even more restrictive by significantly increasing the size of the Quarantia quorum required to grant approval. From 1323, membership of the Great Council became permanent and hereditary only.

Henceforth – not for the first time – the doge would be elected by a small elite, and ordinary Venetians would be excluded from the process: a new legislation stipulated that selection must be carried out not by the Great Council as a whole, but by eleven electors chosen by that council. In this way the democratic Republic changed into an oligarchy, but while this represented a serious infringement of the people's rights, it also greatly

Opposite: Marco Polo began his life of intrepid exploring when he accompanied his father Nicolò and his uncle Matteo along the Silk Road and on their ambassadorial visit to Kublai Khan, the Great Khan of the Mongols.

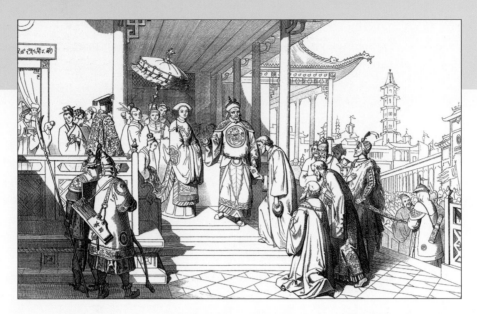

IN 1265 TWO ENTERPRISING VENETIAN MERCHANTS, the Polo brothers, who already had commercial interests in the Crimea on the northern shores of the Black Sea, set out to investigate the markets of the Asian interior. Relying on information and maps from other travellers, they made the gruelling journey across central Asia and visited the Great Khan of the Mongols, Kublai Khan. This unusually enlightened ruler sent them back west with a message to the Pope, since the Mongols were interested in a pact with the Christians against the Muslims. Six years after their first expedition the Polos set out again to take the embassy of Pope Gregory X to the Mongol emperor. This time they were accompanied by Nicolo's seventeen-year-old son, Marco.

In his famous account of his travels Marco Polo describes seeing, on the shores of the Caspian Sea, fountains gushing with a dark substance that could be used in lamps. This 'black gold' became a commodity that governments in later centuries used

MARCO POLO: MARVELS FROM THE EAST

to manipulate economies and go to war over. The Polos crossed the present Pakistan and Afghanistan following the ancient Silk Road, the route by which silk, tea and other exotic oriental products reached the distant Mediterranean on camel trains. At last, after some four years of travelling, the Venetian adventurers arrived in Peking (now Beijing).

Having entered the emperor's good graces, Marco was sent on missions to various parts of the Empire and to Tibet, Burma and Indo-China. For three years he administered Yangzhou and became closely acquainted with the life and customs of the people. So useful, in fact, were the Venetians to Kublai Khan that he could not bear to let them go home.

The three intrepid merchants eventually returned to Venice in

1295, twenty-four years after their departure. On their return Marco Polo knocked at the door of the family home, but as he was dressed in rough Tartar clothes, he was not recognized by his family at first. A feast was then prepared, during which Marco Polo dramatically cut open his rough travelling clothes with a knife and poured out diamonds and precious stones, to the amazement of all around.

While imprisoned by the Genoese after the naval battle of Curzola, Marco dictated the story of his travels to his cell-mate, a Pisan man of letters named Rusticello. The result was *Il Milione*, in which tales of the fabulous are interwoven with rigorous observations. For a long time it was the only source of information for the Western world on the Far East. Freed from prison in 1299, Marco Polo returned to Venice and died there twenty-five years later. On his deathbed he is supposed to have said: 'I wrote not even half of what I saw.'

contributed to the city's stability and the endurance of the Republic
for many centuries. However, these measures quashed so many political
aspirations that discontent became inevitable and ultimately led to rebellion.

Externally, relations with the pope continued to be unstable and
excommunications were the order of the day. Four years into the fifteenth
century, Giovanninus da Mosto was absolved from major excommunication
by Pope Benedict XI for having traded with the religious enemy – he had
sold a galley and some timber in Alexandria. The relationship between
Venetians and Muslims – especially, later, the Ottoman Turks – was always
ambivalent. War and (illegal) trade alternated constantly, and Giovanninus
was probably just unlucky to have been caught.

The economic policy of the Venetian Republic in the Adriatic
consisted of ensuring that all goods passed through its own markets. Ships
and merchants from all nations could go to Venice, but the merchandise
had to be unloaded there before its onward journey to mainland Europe.
In 1308 the Venetians saw the chance of strengthening their control over the
River Po, the key to traffic in northern Italy, by seizing Ferrara. Intervening
in an internal quarrel over succession, they sent in troops and took over
Castel Tedaldo, the fortress that dominated the bridge over the Po. Reviving
an earlier claim to Ferrara by the papacy, Pope Clement V reacted with
lightning swiftness and issued a menacing interdict against Venice:

> *If within thirty days the Ferrarese are not left free, the doge, his counsellors,*
> *all Venetians and every inhabitant of the Venetian dominion shall be*
> *immediately excommunicated. Also those who bring supplies and*
> *merchandise of any sort to Venice, or who buy goods and any other thing*
> *from the Venetians, shall be immediately excommunicated. The doge and*
> *all Venetians shall not be admitted as witnesses, nor shall they be eligible*
> *to make wills and their children shall not be admitted to any ecclesiastic*
> *benefit until the fourth generation. The prelates and ecclesiastics of all*
> *degrees in a range of ten miles of Venice shall depart within ten days,*
> *or suffer excommunication themselves. The doge, the counsellors and all*
> *Venetians, if they do not obey within ten days, shall be servants of those*
> *who capture them and all their goods shall belong to those who enter into*
> *their possession.*

Dante, no admirer, described this pope as a 'lawless pastor of foul behaviour'.
Having been brought up as a Catholic, I had always wondered what
excommunication was all about. As a child I imagined it meant being sent to
hell, but Clement V's words suggest that power and financial considerations
were of far greater weight. Subsequently all those who felt they had been
damaged by Venice's commercial supremacy felt free to plunder Venetian

merchants, and Castel Tedaldo was snatched back. Venice, undaunted, negotiated with Verona to use a route that bypassed Ferrara.

Hard on the heels of the interdict came the conspiracy of Bajamonte Tiepolo. Having personal reasons for detesting Doge Pietro Gradenigo, Tiepolo took advantage of the anger that the Locking of the Great Council had aroused among Venetians and in 1310 hatched a plot to unseat him. It involved members of the patrician Querini, Badoer, Doro and other families, including one Piero da Mosto. Forty years earlier Piero's father, Marco, had been one of the electors of Doge Lorenzo Tiepolo, which explained his current sympathy for Bajamonte.

The insurgents set out armed to the teeth one night, with the intention of attacking the Doge's Palace. But the authorities, forewarned, had brought in reinforcements. As it happened, they were not needed. While the disaffected party was passing along the Mercerie, a main artery connecting the Rialto and San Marco, an old woman dropped a stone mortar from her windowsill on to the head of the standard-bearer of Bajamonte's group, killing him. The conspirators, thrown into confusion, fled. In the palazzo where I now live there is a print that shows the doge in the forefront of the battle in St Mark's Square; his angry face seems to jut

Above: Canaletto's depiction of St Mark's Basin (1729) shows the *Bucintoro* out on the lagoon, indicating an important celebration involving the whole city. Regattas and ceremonies have been a major part of Venetian life for hundreds of years and are heartily conserved to maintain the connection between Venice and the lagoon in a cultural, as well as physical, context.

out of the picture. I was always struck by his ferocious expression, but the thought that a mortar accidentally dropped by an old woman had brought a potentially bloody revolt to an early end never fails to reassure me.

Of the conspirators, Querini was killed on the scene, Badoer was captured, tortured and sentenced to death, while Tiepolo and the other survivors withdrew to their headquarters on the other side of the Grand Canal. They then negotiated an amnesty – granted on condition that they went into exile for life.

Although the rebels were defeated, the danger to the State had been real enough. It was at this time that the Council of Ten was instituted to keep an eye out for any future social unrest and deal with it promptly. It is said that the famous Venetian regatta, too, was introduced at this point to distract the people from any thoughts of a backlash. The Bourbon rulers of Naples in the eighteenth century were to adopt a similar strategy, known as *forca, farina e festa* – gallows, flour and feasts.

SHIPS, SAILORS AND HARD TACK

Innovations in sailing techniques now made commercial navigation possible all year round – the port of Venice had previously closed over the winter. There were also developments in the ships themselves. During Venice's thousand-year history Mediterranean navigation was based mainly on *galee*

(galleys), which evolved into *galeazze* (galleasses) and *navi* (ships). Galleys and galleasses were long boats with both sails and oars, while ships were large, round-bottomed and powered only by sail.

The galley was used in battle, and in large fleets for trade. It was reliable because it could always use oars when there was no wind, and since it had a large crew, including twenty-seven benches of oarsmen, it could always defend itself. Oars were also handy for manoeuvring in port, for steering back into the wind and for rapid movements in combat. A major innovation came about in the sixteenth century with the large *galera grossa* (trading-galley), able to transport about 250 tonnes of merchandise below deck. It was about six times as long as it was wide, as against the eight-to-one ratio of the war galley.

Left: The entrance to the
Arsenale, guarded by
marble lions brought
from Greece. Its prolific
production line, based
on rigorous organization
and discipline, ensured
Venice's superiority on
the seas.

War galleys were built longer and narrower so that the sides could provide space for more oars and therefore increase the vessel's power. It had three masts with lateen sails, and used oars in emergencies, with just one oar per bench, handled by three to five oarsmen. With a crew of two hundred – oarsmen and gunners – this type of vessel could achieve a speed of about eight knots. One cannon was placed towards the bow, where the battering ram used to be situated, while others were positioned on the sides, which contained small gun-ports. The main deck was kept free for manoeuvring the sails, while thirty-two benches of oarsmen were situated under the deck.

In the Battle of Lepanto against the Turks in 1571, galleasses were used for the first time. Although hard to manoeuvre, they delivered a sixteenth-century version of 'shock and awe' with the force of their firepower and won the day for the Venetians and their allies.

The *navi* (oarless round-bottomed sailing ships) needed fewer crew members and could therefore carry more than the galleys, whether ammunition and cannons or trading goods. They could travel alone, unlike the galleys, which sailed in convoy.

Provisions for long voyages consisted mainly of bean soup, fresh or salted meat, cheese and the Arsenale bakeries' speciality of hard tack or *biscotto* (biscuit-bread) – bread hardened (and thus given a longer shelf life) by being baked twice. It was considered the best in all the Mediterranean, and ships from other countries would stock up with it in Venice. The precious recipe was lost at the end of the eighteenth century, when the only baker in possession of it died suddenly. In 1821 in Candia (Crete) a bricked-up storehouse in a Venetian fortress, which had been abandoned for over one hundred and fifty years, was opened and a great store of biscuit-bread found inside was still edible – to the delight of the population, which was suffering a famine at the time.

Free sailors – as they all were before the mid-sixteenth century, when convicts started to be used – were allowed almost 700 grams of biscuits a day, four cups of wine, a bowl of soup, half a kilo of pork or beef, Sardinian cheese and tuna-fish in oil. The passengers enjoyed better food: Malmsey wine, lettuce, mutton, mortadella sausage, cheeses, tripe, Genoese cakes, thrushes, geese and quails – all of them spiced, of course.

The ships had to call at a port to take on fresh water every two or three days because it quickly went brackish. For meat, livestock was often kept in a pen to the stern. Scurvy, the plague of all ocean-going sailing ships, was totally unknown in the Venetian navy, possibly because the ships carried lemon juice as well as wine and vinegar.

The oarsmen themselves had no other accommodation than their benches, on which they rowed, ate and slept. It was rare for them all to row together; they were used in rotation so that each man always rowed at his full strength. But although arduous, the life of an oarsman offered guaranteed wages and the opportunity to engage in a little trade on the side without paying duties. Before setting out on a voyage the oarsmen received four months' pay to keep their families going while they were away. A member of my own family, Nicolò da Mosto, was one of the official paymasters and recruiters; a painting in the Arsenale Museum shows him with bags full of coins under the table.

In times of war ships underwent some remarkable metamorphoses. Here is the story of an early sixteenth-century vessel that bore the name of my family, *Nave Mosta*: one of the four largest in Venice at that time, owned by Francesco and Bortolomio da Mosto, it was a 150-tonne caravel with a hundred and ten men, forty-five of them sailors. In 1504, on a voyage from Cyprus to Corfu with a cargo of salt, the anchor and hawser were lost and the shrouds damaged. Back at the Arsenale in Venice it was loaned a replacement hawser but was then requisitioned by the government for the war against the Turks. In 1507 Francesco da Mosto, the captain, died in combat. But the ship's life was not over and in 1521, seized by the Turks along with a valuable cargo of Malmsey wine, it was pressed into the Turkish fleet.

Before the end of the thirteenth century Venetians had already sailed out into the Atlantic in privately owned ships and made for the North Sea, in competition with other seapowers, including the Genoese. They promptly set up the first regular shipping service to Flanders, calling at the ports of Bruges and London; in 1319 five Venetian galleys docked at Southampton. Routes were also established to the East, pushing on overland beyond the Black Sea in search of new markets, as Marco Polo had done.

In those days navigational aids were not sophisticated; latitude had to be worked out from the stars, and for longitude there were only parchment maps and descriptions by earlier navigators, together with continual reference to the coastline. A notable example of a navigation diary, the *Portolano del Mediterraneo* (Mediterranean Port Guide) was written by Alvise da Mosto, a fifteenth-century navigator and my favourite ancestor:

> *If you want to go from Alexandria to Gozzo di Crede, sail between the west and northwest, and more towards the northwest you will come to Gozzo, and it is 500 miles. And if you then wish to sail from Alexandria to the mountains, sail from the west towards northwest, and you will come safely to Resaltino, and from the above-mentioned place to this it is 500 miles. If you want to go from Barberia to Resaltin sail for the west, and you will come soon to the shallows of Africa, it is 1000 miles. If you sail from Resaltin between west and northwest, you would come to Malta and then to Lampedusa: it is in all 800 miles.*

THE MEDIEVAL COMMODITIES MARKET

FOR MOST OF ITS HISTORY the Republic, with its immense web of trading connections, its political alliances and its strategically intelligent use of the sword, continued to grow in economic status. Its strength lay not just in its beautiful glass, or even in its magnificent silks and wool, or in its indispensable salt, but in its ability to acquire and transport goods that everyone wanted from distant lands. Foreigners were everywhere in Venice: the Rialto, the centre of all traffic, teemed with Jewish, Dutch, Tuscan, French, Genoese and German merchants, to name but a few. The Serenissima presented an image of prosperity and opulence to the world, which envied the city for its material and artistic wealth. The fourteenth-century poet Petrarch, doing his bit for public relations, wrote that the wines of Venice sparkled in the glasses of Breton fishermen and that Venetian honey was served even in Russian homes.

The demand for spices in medieval Europe was enormous. Pepper, nutmeg, ginger, cinnamon, galangal, cloves, star anise and saffron were all objects of desire. People were ready to pay exorbitant prices for such commodities, which could be used to conserve meat, to give flavour to the monotonous and frugal dishes of the day and to combat infections. It is therefore no surprise that the Venetians cornered the spice trade, which in turn influenced the development of the Western financial powers.

The centres of production were mainly in the East Indies and southern China, places where few Westerners except missionaries travelled. So it was Malay and Arab traders who transported spices, along with sugar cane, perfumed essences, madder dye, lac, gum tragacanth, alum (to fix dyes), silk, pearls and precious stones. After arrival in Persian Gulf or Red Sea ports, the goods would be taken overland by caravan to the borders of the Christian world. Constantinople was a rich entrepôt, where the Byzantines amassed these treasures from Trebizond on the Black Sea, and from Antioch and Alexandria on the Muslim Mediterranean.

Venice played a dominant role in this world trade, and it became a daily custom to distribute small coupons showing the average prices of spices on the Rialto market; the spices themselves were used as a means of payment when cash was short. The wholesale trade, reserved for the great bankers rather than the spice merchants, used an auction system: at the Rialto offers were whispered into people's ears, and the *messeri del pepe* (pepper officers) became a category of State-appointed brokers.

But after 1498 everything changed. The ambitions of fifteenth-century Portugal were embodied in King Henry the Navigator, the great scholar of geography and ancient wisdom, who sponsored expeditions along the African coasts, including those of my ancestor Alvise da Mosto. His successor Manuel I sent Bartolomeo Diaz down the west coast of Africa and round the fateful Cape of Storms, subsequently renamed the Cape of Good Hope. In his wake went Vasco da Gama, who ventured as far as India and beyond, into the heart of the spice world. Financed by Florentine bankers, in 1504 da Gama brought home huge cargoes of pepper and other spices, which made a profit of about 400 per cent. It was Lisbon that now attracted the trade of northern Europe, causing a crisis in Venice, where the banks crashed.

It was in 1329 that the Senate first decided to charter State galleys to the highest bidder, one voyage at a time, on fixed routes. Rigorous laws stipulated the limits for cargoes, regulated crews and provisions, and laid down the duties to be paid. Even the largest ships had to be able to anchor in front of St Mark's and delivered all kinds of merchandise, including slaves, to the Rialto market. A certain Bartolomeo da Mosto and his kinsman Bernardo got into trouble. One was tried for salt-smuggling and the other, captain of the *Napoli della Romania*, was fined for some wrongdoing, imprisoned for six months and banned from public office in perpetuity.

All through the Middle Ages and beyond, convoys set out at specific times of the year, always travelling to the same destinations: beyond Constantinople to the Black Sea and then to Romania or to trade with the Tartars and Russians in the Crimea; to Cyprus and Syria in the East; to Alexandria in Egypt; and passing through Tripoli and Tangier to touch Spain before heading north to Antwerp and London. It was a kind of 'scheduled service' transporting all kinds of goods. In Venice these convoys were called *mude*, which may derive from *mute*, meaning 'sets' or 'herds'. In 1420 there were about four thousand Venetian mercantile ships ploughing the seas with over fifteen thousand sailors on board.

As far as commerce with the mainland was concerned, in the early fourteenth century the Scaligero family of Verona had begun to threaten Venetian interests from their own city to Padua and Treviso. Treviso was important for the trade routes to the north and had been the first mainland city to succumb to Venetian dominion. After some hard diplomacy, the Scaligeri were persuaded to curtail their ambitions, and signed a peace treaty with the Republic in 1339.

I see from family records that daily life for the da Mostos, with a range of responsibilities typical of a patrician family, proceeded as usual. One of them had to oversee canal dredging in front of the Doge's Palace; a galley owner asked for exemption from import duty on cloth returned from Alexandria since he had already paid export tax on it; an adviser to the doge participated in collective decisions on the number of horses and crossbowmen to be sent to the various colonies; Sister Marchesina da Mosto, abbess of the convent of San Zaccaria, had a new bell cast with suitable pomp and ceremony. Bono da Mosto is remembered as a loyal and upright administrator of justice, a *savio* and member of the Council of Ten, whose name appears as witness in the act confirming Marco Corner, later doge, as Count of Zara on the Dalmatian coast after it had been forced into submission. Not all of my family, however, were such model citizens. Benedetto da Mosto was sentenced to six months in prison for wounding a spice trader; later, appointed to guard the Castle of Serravalle, he abandoned his post and returned to Venice, for which he was fined 100 ducats.

Opposite: Venice's strategic maritime and diplomatic skills brought it prestigious trading connections and the Republic successfully tapped into the enormous demand for spices in medieval Europe.

THE GHETTO: JEWISH LIFE IN VENICE

———

THE JEWS OCCUPIED A PROMINENT POSITION in Venetian trade but, as in many places, were not universally popular.

They had originally lived on the island of Spinalunga, renamed Giudecca to reflect their presence. But during the Middle Ages the authorities ordered them – ostensibly for their own safety – to reside only in the area near the bronze foundries, and not to leave it at night or during Christian festivals. The district was called the Ghetto – either from a word meaning a casting, or from one that signified a chain, for the place was chained, locked up and guarded at night. The word 'ghetto' has passed into many languages to indicate an area whose inhabitants, in modern times not necessarily Jews, are separated from the rest of society. Only with the arrival of Napoleon in 1797 was the Ghetto unlocked so that Jews could circulate freely.

Limitated ground space meant the houses became mini-skyscrapers to provide sufficient living space. The community included butchers and bakers, who prepared food in accordance with Jewish tradition. All judicial controversies were resolved within the community itself.

Further restrictions on Venetian Jews included the mandatory wearing of red or black hats, and a list of the trades or professions they were allowed to enter. Commerce, the selling of secondhand goods and moneylending were all acceptable, the last of these being in any case forbidden to Christians. Jews were also allowed to take degrees in medicine at Padua University, and to practise as doctors freely throughout the Republic.

Above left: An old synagogue on top of houses in the area traditionally known as the Ghetto.

The years 1347 and 1348 were terrible ones for the city: it suffered an earthquake, a series of exceptionally low tides that made navigation difficult even on the Grand Canal and, finally, the Black Death set in. The plague had begun in India in 1332, swept through the Tartar army besieging the trading station of Caffa in the Crimea, and was probably brought to Italy on a Venetian galley in autumn 1347. Venice was one of the most densely populated cities in medieval Europe, with over a hundred and thirty thousand inhabitants, but in just eighteen months it lost nearly three-fifths of them. And the plague continued through Europe.

In mid-century the Genoese began to exert pressure on Black Sea trade again. Another war broke out between the two cities; this time it was Venice who enjoyed the protection of the Byzantine Empire. The Venetians augmented their plague-depleted crews with Greek and Dalmatian mercenaries, but these men's main interest was pillaging. A succession of naval battles occurred throughout the Adriatic, Aegean and Mediterranean; near the Dalmatian coast the Venetian ships were caught off guard and more than five thousand soldiers were taken prisoner to be displayed in Genoa as war booty. A compromise peace was brokered by Milan in 1355. Back in Venice, Andrea Dandolo was succeeded as doge by a man whose name has become a byword for treachery.

VENICE PRESERVED: A COUP AND A NEAR-INVASION

Doge Marin Falier was conceded his last wish, to distribute 2000 lire to the poor and for good works, on 17 April 1355. Significantly, it was a Friday – Friday the 17th being regarded superstitiously as unlucky in Italy. The execution was performed at sunset, at the top of the same stone staircase where he had been sworn in as doge. His *corno* and insignia of office were removed before he was beheaded. The bloody head was then displayed by the executioner to the people gathered before the Doge's Palace: 'Behold, everybody, that justice has been done to the traitor.' The body remained on show for a day and a night before being buried in an unmarked grave. So how had Marin Falier's dogeship come to such a bitter end?

One of the leading figures of the day in Venice, Falier was, typically, an elder statesman of over seventy when elected doge. The King of Bohemia had appointed him knight and counsellor. He was Count of Valmareno, Lord of the Castle of Fregone, and owned lands near Padua and Ferrara. He had held many public and military posts, had led important embassies and been a *condottiere* (mercenary leader) on land and sea. He was *savio* on several occasions, but still found time to engage in commerce: cargoes of spices, corn, timber, alum and cloth were transported for him on galleys. He was, it would seem, the very model of a medieval civic dignitary.

Right: *Molo e riva degli* Schiavoni by Ippolito Caffi (1864) shows the two granite columns outside the Doge's Palace that Doge Falier unknowingly walked between on his arrival in Venice.

When he became doge in 1354, the forty-one electors included a certain Bono da Mosto. As Falier was then ambassador to the pope at Avignon, he was ceremoniously brought to Venice on the *Bucintoro*. In thick fog, the boat moored by the Piazzetta, where Falier disembarked and unwittingly passed between the two columns that were the place of execution – a bad omen.

The new doge had a beautiful second wife called Aluica, a relative of Doge Pietro Gradenigo. Falier was outraged when a young nobleman named Michele Steno wrote a libellous verse impugning his wife's morals. Insult was added to injury when the Quarantia took previous good character into account and pronounced only a light sentence. This may have contributed to imminent events – revenge may have been on his mind, not just on Steno but on the authorities whom he felt had let him down. Certainly Steno's action may have been influenced by his own family's quarrel with the Faliers: a Steno had deflowered a Falier girl and was then forced to marry her.

However, the principal cause of Falier's attempted coup was probably political ambition. Throughout Italy, communes were being transformed into signorie and principalities; the dogeship and its surrounding oligarchy seemed meagre in comparison, and Falier craved all the powers of a signore for himself. The main aim of the conspiracy was probably to establish a kind of dictatorship.

The da Mosto connection ran deeper than mere electoral support. A year earlier Falier had travelled to Ferrara with Renier da Mosto to settle differences that had arisen between the two cities. The pair also went to the Malatesta court of Rimini to arrange a peace settlement with the Signore of Fermo. Numerous other forebears of mine were also involved directly or indirectly with Falier. In Venice he shared a court-yard with the da Mostos. Six years previously he had acted as peacemaker in a dispute between Renier and his son Pietro on the one hand, and Paolo Morosini on the other, over the estate of Andrea da Mosto. Andrea had married Isabeta Falier; their daughter had married Paolo Morosini's father, Alessandro. Isabeta later became the executor of the doge's much talked about widow. Another da Mosto, Polo, married Cataruzza Falier, a distant cousin of this doge, but later remarried. It is not clear whether the first wife was dead or not – maybe he found it politic to leave her after the doge had been disgraced and beheaded. As fate would have it, the following year his brother Renier, Falier's former diplomatic colleague, was appointed to the inquiry into the doge's conspiracy and was one of the special additional members (*giunta*) of the Council of Ten that sentenced Falier. Another da Mosto, Renier's nephew Pietro, from whom my branch of the family descends, was also one of the Council of Ten and 'demonstrated his zeal towards his country on the occasion of the conspiracy', according to notes found in the Venetian State Archives.

The plot was uncovered thanks to the indiscretion of at least one of the conspirators. Eleven of them were hanged, three were given life sentences, one a year in prison, one banished to Candia (Crete), five more banished, and thirty-one pardoned with special admonitions. Yet another da Mosto, Stefano by name, took part in the affair; he came off relatively well, suffering only banishment.

In May 1355 the Council of Ten, in gratitude to God and St Mark for saving the State from the Falier conspiracy, decreed that an annual procession should be held, led by the doge and culminating in a solemn Mass celebrated in St Mark's. It is said that a cloth, originally white and later red symbolizing the blood from the executioner's block, was placed on the high altar of the Basilica on Good Friday.

In December 1366, by decree of the Council of Ten, the place on the wall of the Sala del Maggior Consiglio where Falier's effigy should have been placed was painted and inscribed: *Hic fuit locus ser Marini Faletri decapitati pro crimine proditionis* (This would have been the place of Marin Falier, beheaded for the crime of treason). After a fire in the Doge's Palace in 1577 a black veil was hung in the same place with the words: *Hic est locus Marini Faletri decapitati pro criminibus* (This is the place of Marin Falier, beheaded for crimes).

As a da Mosto I have to wonder: one of our family promoted him and was his close colleague, two were related through marriage, two others of this period conjures up fascinating images of postwar events in the run-up to the peace treaty and includes details of my otherwise unknown ancestor, ambassador Jacopo da Mosto:

The ferocious invaders had been dying in prison, day by day, for the last few months. After the hunger of the siege, when the last cats and then rats had been skinned, the last leathers boiled, their stomachs unable to absorb bread, they surrendered, and even those who had survived now fell prey to strange diseases. This must have been why the Ligurian [Genoese] ambassadors had proved more malleable in recent days; every time the messenger arrived from Genoa, soaked in his own sweat and that of his horse, he would present to the leader of the delegation in Turin not only invitations to press for as many concessions as possible, but also letters from patricians stating how urgent it was that the boys of

JACOPO DA MOSTO AND THE TURIN PEACE SETTLEMENT

'79 should return as soon as possible, those boys who had set off with banners held high and who were now mere wraiths. Jacopo da Mosto had no doubt that the peace treaty must be signed at once.

In the short term our city, after all the blood that had been spilt, may have been no better off than Genoa, but in the long term, we would recover better than the Ligurians, who were traditionally only united in war, lords of a strip of mountainous territory, morbidly avaricious, even to the detriment of their own fellow-countrymen. Our economic policy, on the other hand, was decided by the Senate of the Republic and, once agreed, it was respected throughout the Mediterranean and northern Europe. The interests of individual families always yielded to those of the State, sometimes under compulsion

but usually through clear conviction. And meanwhile Treviso had been reconquered, with its fertile lands, Padua punished, while all six sestieri of Candia [Crete] were once again sending us their oil and slaves and all the sugar amassed in their ware-houses, as soon as it came from the plantations of the Corner family and the other Veneto-Cypriot land-owners.

The Venetians still needed to pursue the policy of gaining control over the East: recover Dalmatia, defeat the king of Hungary, obtain supremacy on the mainland, ensuring that they never again suffer a surprise attack from a new Scaligero [of Milan], or from an envious and treacherous Paduan. But there was no question of taking on the Genoese now, with their own young people decimated and all their neighbours hostile; they would be doomed to failure.

To convince the more reluctant patricians to accept the treaty, Jacopo attempted a pre-emptive strike. As soon as he heard of a barbaric

participated in sentencing him to death and one was exiled for taking part in the conspiracy. Just a series of strange coincidences?

However dramatic the Falier affair may have been, it had little influence on the Republic's foreign policies. After the 1355 truce with Genoa, in order to stabilize its confines and its colonies Venice had to deal with the dukes of Austria, the patriarch of Aquileia, the city of Padua and the Hungarians, all of whom had their sights set on the Dalmatian coast and mainland expansion. During this period Venice also strengthened its defences against pirates. When Lorenzo Celsi, captain of the Gulf of Venice, decision by the Genoese to starve their Venetian prisoners, to make them share the sufferings of the Genoese under siege in Chioggia, he realized that the pro-war party in Venice would have a powerful argument to make their lion close his book of peace; so the diplomatic boat now sped eastwards along the Po, bearing with it Jacopo's letter to the Senate.

But the most pressing matter was the exchange of prisoners: had the Venetians heard that our lads were being starved by the Genoese? If they wanted peace, why let them suffer and die in enemy prisons? If they wanted war, why not exchange men still able to serve their country for the Genoese skeletons in the dungeons?

Jacopo knew all about politics; at thirty-seven, after a period spent in his father's *mude* trading with Jaffa, he had already served the Republic as the captain of the Castle of Modon, which, with Coron, constituted the 'eyes of the Republic'; there one heard all that happened in the East and most of what was discussed in the Doge's Palace. His letter would make the mediator's task much easier; and the Venetians would do far better out of the peace of Savoy, in the long run, than the subjects of St George – the Genoese.

'God must have given you his grace,' was the cheery comment of Almorò da Mosto, his friend both in battle and over a flask of Malmsey. He had been chosen by the Senate to tell Jacopo the news that his 'most humble proposal' had passed with sixty votes in favour and only twelve against (the other voters abstained). Almorò went on:

I got here from Turin this morning at five o'clock and they didn't even want to open the Susa gate to me, and I find you still up. How will you manage? In two hours' time you're due to tell these Genoese dogs that they'll have to allow our young men *to leave under Savoy escort if they want an immediate peace. Before you go and get a couple of hours' sleep, you must let me drink a jar of Cyprus water, two measures of Cyprus water and three of Malmsey, for me, for you and for the two girls who tried to keep me in the boat but who then insisted on following me and who are now waiting for me in bed, in our chamber.*

Almorò was chewing cinnamon mixed with some other exotic devilry from Persia; there were many in Venice who relished these forbidden delights, but he was probably the only one who drank Malmsey wine on top of it, mixed not with water but with the much stronger Cyprus wine. Jacopo embraced him, wept, knelt in front of the lion of Istrian marble that hung on the wall, drank the last drops from the cask that his friend had almost drained in the meantime, and then went to his room. The next day the treaty was signed.

was elected doge he was on patrol in the Adriatic. Piero da Mosto and eleven other noblemen went out in a galley to bring him back ceremoniously to the city. (This doge's father apparently gave up wearing anything on his head to avoid having to raise his hat to his son.) But if the pirates were temporarily under control, the hinterland remained unstable: twelve noblemen, including a da Mosto, took a force of sixty crossbowmen to defend Treviso against the Hungarians.

And still the trouble with Genoa rumbled in the background, surfacing from time to time in overt hostilities. It gave Doge Andrea Contarini, who was elected in 1368, no respite. The present argument concerned control of the island of Tenedos in the Aegean, and of the Dardanelles strait leading to Constantinople and the Black Sea. When Venice occupied the island in 1376, war broke out.

The commander of a Venetian fleet that surrendered a year or two later, Vettor Pisani, was imprisoned on his return home, accused of lack of resolve. In August 1379 the Genoese, in alliance with the Paduans, took Chioggia and, alarmingly, advanced as far as the island of Poveglia, only 5 kilometres (3 miles) from St Mark's. The whole city was mobilized, and ships were equipped with the assistance of noblemen and merchants who donated goods, jewellery, gold and silver to the cause. The people's assembly met in the Basilica and agreed that in the name of the Miracle of St Mark the Evangelist Venice must be saved; the sailors demanded that Vettor Pisani, 'leader and father of all the sailors of Venice', be released from prison.

On 18 September 1379, one of a number of observers placed strategically along the coast, Fantino da Mosto, *podestà* (governor) of Pirano in Istria, sent a letter to the doge containing information on the movements of the Genoese fleet in the northern Adriatic. In December the doge and Vettor Pisani, now a free man, blockaded Chioggia and the Genoese were left isolated. After six months of appalling conditions the starving Genoese surrendered and the Venetians regained control of the Adriatic. Following the peace treaty of 1381, brokered by the Count of Savoy in Turin, thirty new Venetian families – those who had contributed most to the war effort – were admitted to the Great Council. Neither side had actually won the war, but Venice was to win the peace – its economic resurgence matched Genoa's decline, from which it would never recover.

At the end of the fourteenth century the troubled dogeship of Antonio Venier began with the plague – which carried off his predecessor, Michele Morosini – and ended with the plague, almost like sinister seals of office. In between, there were strategic territorial gains on the Italian mainland and further afield, and astute diplomatic moves to further Venetian commerce.

One of Venier's first acts was the reconstruction of Chioggia, half-destroyed by the war. In the East Venice reacquired Corfu, which it had lost in 1221. An extremely important base for control of the southern Adriatic, it remained under Venetian rule until the end of the Republic. Favours and privileges for Venetian merchants were obtained from the kings of England and Granada. On the mainland, through artful shifts of allegiance among the various rival states, Venice managed to occupy the Treviso area, essential for unfettered movement through the Po valley. On that occasion Paolo da Mosto, leader of a punitive expedition into Trevisan territory after Mestre had been attacked, devastated the land and returned home with numerous prisoners and cattle. Venice received complaints from the Signore of Padua

QVISQVIS AD INSIGNEM TVMVLVM TVA LVMINA FLECTIS,
INGENTEM CVIVS CINERES HÆC MARMORA SERVANT,
CONTEMPLARE DVCEM, PRINCEPS HIC ILLE PER OMNEM

Left: Doge Venier's tomb in Santi Giovanni e Paolo. His wife, Agnese da Mosto, is buried beside him. This church was built on land donated by Doge Jacopo Tiepolo in the thirteenth century and the funerals of the doges were held here.

THERE WERE TWO FORMS OF GUILDS or 'schools' in Venice. One consisted of the Confraternities or Schools of Artisans, whose trades were regulated by the government. They bore the name of the patron saint of their craft, and were often affiliated to churches. The Scuola di San Rocco, with its splendid paintings by Tintoretto, is an example. The other kind, such as the *Compagnia della Calza* (Company of the Stocking), were recreational associations of patrician gentlemen, whose object, proclaimed in their statutes, was not only to foster brotherhood but also to organize festivals and shows.

Licensed by the Council of Ten, they had a variety of colourful names: Peacocks, Powerful, Immortal, Peaceful, Fortunate, Modest, Gardeners, Kitchen Gardeners, Triumphant, Virtuous, Moderate, Valorous, Courteous,

FESTIVITIES AND GAMES

Sempiternal, Bright and even Hoseless – the fashion of long stockings or hose having just arrived from France. The Companies were distinguished by the colours of their stockings. Some would be divided into two colours lengthwise, while others were a single colour. The stockings would bear the coat-of-arms and motto of the Company embroidered in gold thread and often adorned with precious stones. On the Company's gondola the cloth cover of the *felze* (cabin) displayed the same coat-of-arms.

The games played on public holidays included *pallamaglio* and *pallacorda* – essentially, football and tennis. The former was the famous Florentine game, from which the term 'pell-mell' derives (it was probably a fairly rough,

fast-moving affair), as does the London street named Pall Mall, where a version of it was once played. What we might call the first football pitch in Venice was the Campo San Giacomo dell'Orio; the two teams, distinguished by the white or black feathers of their caps, were allowed to use only their feet to move the ball. Calle della Racchetta takes its name from the field where *pallacorda* was played. The *Trattato del Giuoco della Palla* (Treatise on the Ball-game) by Antonio Scanio da Salò, published in Venice in 1555 (there is a copy in the museum at Wimbledon in London), contains a description of the game. The game was played by ambassadors and papal nuncios, emperors and kings. Young Frederick August of Saxony seems to have been the best player of all – and also the most generous, tipping the caretaker of the field four ducats a day.

but stated it knew nothing about the affair, blaming the Signore of Verona.

Doge Venier is remembered most for his dogged insistence on equality before the law. When his playboy son Alvise, who had been sent to prison, fell ill in the dank air of the dungeon, the doge refused to have him released. Despite the pleas of the boy's mother, Agnese da Mosto, and even the judges, the young man was left to die. This terrible and even unnatural act of justice weighed heavily on the doge, whose own death is said to have been from *condormia*, the stress of inflexible judgement due to extreme integrity. But perhaps some good came out of this tragedy. Laws were subsequently passed stipulating that doctors must visit prisoners every two weeks to check their state of health; later it became mandatory for magistrates to visit them as well, in order to hear their complaints. Even in the modern world such rights are by no means universal; despite the unyielding appearance of many of Venice's political systems, in many ways the Republic was ahead of its time.

THE *STATO DA TERRA* – VENICE'S MAINLAND POSSESSIONS

At the beginning of the fifteenth century the *Stato da Terra* (land-state) was becoming a firm reality. In addition to the lagoon and coastal territories of the *Stato da Mar* (sea-state), the Republic now possessed sizeable territories on the mainland. The new century opened with two dogeships that Venice celebrated in grand style.

Michele Steno became an unlikely doge in 1400. In his dissipated youth he had been associated with the Marin Falier affair, and in 1379 he had been imprisoned along with Vettor Pisani for surrendering to the Genoese. The celebrations for his election went on for over a year, with balls, bullfights and games, many of them organized by the Compagnia della Calza – a kind of medieval upper-crust entertainment committee (see opposite). Steno was followed in 1414 by Tommaso Mocenigo, during whose dogeship a great tournament and a jousting match were held in St Mark's Square on the initiative of (and presumably paid for by) the gold-smiths and jewellers of Venice. Among the participants were Nicolò d'Este, Marchese of Ferrara, with two hundred horses and Francesco Gonzaga, Signore of Mantua, with even more. Prizes included a jewel-set gold chain worth 250 gold ducats and a splendid helmet with white ostrich feathers.

Beyond the fun and games and lavish expenditure the period was troubled by a cycle of wars and truces with the usual suspects – the Hungarians, the Turks and the patriarch of Aquileia. But Venice ended up in control of the coasts of Istria, Dalmatia, Albania and Corinth; and, on the mainland, the Friuli region, Feltre, Belluno and the Cadore. During the

Opposite: Detail from a painting (1779–1792) by the Italian artist Gabriele Bella showing the traditional game of *pallacorda*, an early form of tennis, which was hugely popular in Venice on public holidays. My father has a ball from these times – it is slightly smaller than a tennis ball, made of leather and stuffed with wool and horsehair.

hostilities with Hungary, the village of Torre di Mosto had been destroyed and its population expelled, so the da Mosto family brought in new settlers and rebuilt the cornmills. The land was rented out to peasant farmers and shepherds, who paid in kind with grain, vegetables, fruit, timber, cheeses and lambs, as well as special 'tributes' of chickens, geese, eggs and hams. There was hardly any wine after the Hungarians' depradations, so Giovanni da Mosto obliged his tenants to plant rows of vines protected by willows – or pay a heavy fine. But the land was poor and the yields low so, like most of their compatriots, the da Mostos could not live on rents alone but engaged in other areas, such as commerce.

As a marine and mercantile power, Venice based its policies in the Adriatic and the East on the control of ports, trading stations and markets; and similarly, on the mainland, the concern had always been to keep trade routes open. The Republic had created for itself a position as one of the most efficient entrepôts between the Mediterranean coasts and the European landmass. So long as the hinterland had consisted of a host of small, bickering signories, the Republic had had no need of territorial dominion. But as large states began to form as a result of expansionist policies, Venice had to adapt in order to survive. It became, together with Verona under the Scaligeri, Padua under the Carraras, Milan under the Visconti, and the patriarchate of Aquileia, one of the great regional states of fifteenth-century Italy. The Visconti, even though geographically less close than the Carraras, were the most dangerous rivals, especially during the power-crazed Gian Galeazzo Visconti's attempt to bring all northern Italy under his control. However, his death from the plague in 1402 left the way free for Venice.

The patriarch of Aquileia, richest prelate in Italy after the pope, yielded up the castles of the Friuli to Venice, and that was the end of his power. In the lands of the patriarchate the Savorgnan family provided strong support for the Republic, and the intervention of Emperor Sigismund of Hungary, with whom the Venetians were in conflict for control of Dalmatia, provoked a military campaign between 1418 and 1420. On 16 June 1420, while a bolt of lightning in Venice struck the top of the Campanile, setting it on fire, Tristano Savorgnan entered Udine with the standard of St Mark. This brought Venice into possession of further extensive parts of the mainland, covering the Veneto and Friuli Venezia Giulia.

FROM THE SEA TO THE LAND AND VICE VERSA

Francesco Foscari was elected doge in 1423 without the traditional words of presentation to the people, 'if it pleases you'. Sovereignty was now fully in the hands of the Great Council and the patriciate. While the Turks grew into a great seapower, Foscari engaged Venice in further costly and long

Opposite: The tomb of Doge Francesco Foscari in the church of Santa Maria Gloriosa dei Frari, constructed in the fifteenth century. At the time it was known as the *Ca' Granda* (large house) and was the second largest church in Venice.

FRANCESCO FOSCARI: A HAWK WHO FLEW HIGHER THAN FALCONS

TOMMASO MOCENIGO, doge until 1423, focused on Venice's seapower, while his successor, Francesco Foscari, wanted to expand into Italy. Before his death, Mocenigo had drawn up a political testament describing the conditions in which he left the Republic and issuing warnings for the future. In particular he advised against the election of Foscari, whom he considered over-ambitious and obsessed with war, which he thought would only impoverish the State: 'Those who say they want your master Francesco Foscari, I do not understand for what reason, because [he] tells lies and also says many things without any basis, and flies higher than falcons do.'

Foscari was nevertheless elected, and Mocenigo's prophecy came true. To be fair, though, the Italian wars were inevitable since there was no other way to check the Milanese plans to subjugate northern Italy. Although the treaty that ended these wars stretched the Venetian borders as far as the River Adda in Lombardy and to the River Isonzo in Friuli, and also included Ravenna, these gains could not really justify the sacrifices that were made, and ultimately led to a financial crisis. The anti-doge party never let up on Foscari, and it was perhaps indirectly the cause of an attempt on his life, perpetrated by a frustrated and disaffected nobleman, Andrea Contarini, in March 1430. Armed with a dagger, or perhaps an ivory stick, this unbalanced, paranoid individual attacked the doge, wounding him in the nose. The Council of Ten ordered Contarini's hand to be cut off and hung round his neck before he was hanged between the two columns of St Mark. It is said that the sentence would not have been carried out on the poor deranged man if the doge had not lost his temper.

Opposition to Foscari never died down. To disarm it, on three occasions he expressed his wish to renounce the dogeship, but never obtained the agreement of the Ten. These declarations, however, were probably just bluff; when it was suggested that he really should abdicate he would have none of it, and in the end the Council of Ten had to force him out.

drawn-out wars against Milan, which only ended with the peace of Lodi in 1454: once again, Venice added to its mainland possessions. Among the numerous clashes that had taken place all over the Po plain, one was particularly memorable: in 1439 six galleys had been transported overland from the River Adige to Lake Garda, an enormous logistical undertaking that involved two thousand oxen.

This was the age of the explorers, opening up the far reaches of the world to trade in both goods and ideas – ideas that in Venice's case would make the city, and the way it looked, unique in the world. Every great Venetian family had its explorer, and in my house we still have a statue of ours: Alvise da Mosto. On behalf of the Infante of Portugal, Henry the Navigator, at the age of twenty-nine he 'discovered' the Cape Verde Islands off the west coast of Africa. Now that I have turned forty, I have a little boat in which to potter around the lagoon – that is the difference between him and me.

Alvise seems to have been born in 1426 in the family's palace on the Grand Canal, and his early life conformed to the pattern followed by most young patricians of his day. He probably received a minimal education from a tutor or in local schools; then he devoted himself to commerce, embarking at the tender age of thirteen with his cousin Andrea on the galleys that traded with Alexandria, Flanders and Constantinople.

At the customary age of twenty-five, Alvise was admitted to the Great Council, then took the crossbow test in the Arsenale and was appointed 'noble crossbowman' on the large Alexandria galleys. He had quarters in the stern and ate at the table of the commander, Alvise Contarini. His next appointment was as a crossbowman on the Flanders galleys.

So began his sailing career, which was to be a distinguished one. His portrait is in the Sala dello Scudo of the Doge's Palace, where he is named as a 'prince' of nautical skills. He was in distinguished company: also honoured thus was Pietro Loredan, who had defeated the Genoese in the Ligurian seas.

Back in Venice Alvise found his family in desperate financial straits after his father had been banished from the city for some misdemeanour. The explorer wrote later: 'My only thought at that time was to struggle by all means possible to acquire some resources and so to achieve the perfection of honour.'

He decided to return to northern Europe with a cargo of merchandise, and dropped anchor en route in a Portuguese port, where he heard that a commercial expedition was being organized to the Canary Islands. Profit and honour were the potential rewards for risk and a degree of hardship. Young and robust, Alvise had no hesitation in accepting an offer to join the expedition; he was further stimulated by the thought that no Venetian had

Above: Alvise da Mosto, my favourite ancestor.
Left: One of Alvise's expeditions is remembered in this painting, a copy of which hangs in my home (the original is in the Doge's Palace). Alvise was also the first European to describe the group of stars known as the Southern Cross, which are only visible in the southern hemisphere.

ever sailed in those seas. He left his brother Antonio in charge of selling their cargo in Flanders and England while he himself remained in Portugal.

The Infante Don Henry, who was sponsoring the voyage, treated him most cordially and at the beginning of the next year, 1455, Alvise had a caravel of about 45 tonnes fitted out for him, fully equipped and provisioned, under the command of Vicente Diaz. After loading some Spanish horses, woollen cloth, Moorish silks and other goods that he had obtained from the Flanders galleys as barter for the natives, Alvise set sail in March. His account of his voyages described his feelings and the novelties he discovered:

> *As I, Alvise from Ca' da Mosto, am the first that from the most noble city*
> *of Venice have set forth to sail the Ocean beyond the straits of Gibraltar,*

towards the south, to the lands of the Negroes, and having seen many new things on this journey of mine and worthy of notice, it seemed to me worthwhile to expend some labour on this and, as in my memorials from day to day I noted them, so with my pen I shall transcribe them, so that those who come after me will understand in what spirits I was as I sought new and different places, which truly, in comparison with our own, can be called another world.

Their hair is black and they grease it every day with fish-oil; for this reason they stink, which they consider a great sign of gentility. When they caught their first sight of sails or rather ships on the sea they thought they were fish. Others said they were night-time ghosts and were much a-feared. And they said to one another: 'If these are human creatures, how can they travel so far in one night as we cannot do in three days?'

The year after he set off again with three caravels, following the same route as his first voyage and encountering the same reactions from native tribes: 'They wondered at my garments and my whiteness ... Some touched my hands and arms, and rubbed me with spit, to see if my whiteness was dye or real flesh, and seeing that it was flesh they gazed in admiration.'

On this second voyage he endured a tropical storm of unprecedented violence, which raged for a full two days and nights so that he and his companions completely lost their bearings. When it ended, they found themselves in sight of a group of islands of which no record existed. They disembarked and da Mosto sent ten armed men to the highest point, from which they could see that there were eight islands in all. They named them Cape Verde, on account of their luxuriant greenness.

In the 1460s, after writing an account of his expeditions and having compiled his *Portolano*, a Mediterranean port guide, Alvise returned to Venice to run the family's affairs and to engage in commerce and public life. He set up a trading company in Venice, which was soon thriving. Barrels of Malmsey were exchanged in London for pewter objects, chestnuts in Alexandria for sacks of ginger. But cargo was often ruined by salt water and there were frequent disputes over devaluation. Alvise also held various official posts, including that of clerk in the office of the Messetteria, which kept a check on import duties. A law prohibited the removal of goods from the customs office until duty had been paid on them; in the past, unscrupulous cloth merchants had taken merchandise out of the customs office and, when asked to pay the duty, would deny they had ever seen these items.

While Alvise da Mosto and others were 'discovering' new lands off the African Atlantic coast, the Turks had been making new conquests in the Mediterranean. They took Constantinople after a violent assault in 1453, when the Emperor Constantine XI was murdered – along with many thousands of ordinary people, including Venetians – and the Byzantine Empire came to an abrupt end. Its fall was, in part, affected by Doge Foscari's policy of mainland expansion to the detriment of Venetian interests overseas. Ten years later, as the Turks moved inexorably westwards, they seized the Venetian stronghold of Argos in the Morea – too close to the southern Adriatic for comfort. A long war began, the Turks encroached ever closer, and Venice was eventually defeated.

Alvise da Mosto, who had survived service to the Republic in the Turk-infested seas, returned to Venice, where he was elected captain of four armed galleys designated by the Senate for commerce with Alexandria. But business did not prosper – on the homeward journey, late in the season, the ships were severely hampered by high seas; they arrived in Venice after the trade fairs were over and sold less of their cargo than expected.

There was no dashing end for this daredevil adventurer. Having earned respect as an honest administrator, in 1483 Alvise was given the delicate task of travelling to Rovigo and other conquered territories to collect revenues from confiscated estates. It was a role that required the skills of a diplomat and the punctiliousness of a tax collector. As Alvise was widely respected for his intellectual and moral gifts, he would undoubtedly have achieved even greater success had he not died prematurely while on this mission. To this day, no one has found his grave.

But if Venetian foreign affairs and traditional trade were suffering, cultural life was not, for this was the time of the Renaissance. Botticelli, Bramante and Brunelleschi were at work in a flourishing Florence, while Venice became world-famous for printing; Aldo Manuzio, better known as Aldus Manutius, was its principal exponent (see above). Printing soon became a new market for Venice, helping to compensate for the losses incurred in its maritime trade due to Turkish pressure and the new ocean trade routes.

Other da Mostos, clearly less worthy citizens of the Serenissima, are recorded in those years for different reasons. Baldassare, who had been tried for slander twenty years before, was now arrested by the Council of Ten for writing insults against Doge Cristoforo Moro and the State. Francesco was tried for having raped Andriana, daughter of the patrician Alessandro Barbaro, then he married her a few years later. Valerio, who like Alvise worked at the Messetteria, was tried for embezzlement and, as a result, banned from the Great Council for five years and from holding public office in perpetuity. Natale was arrested and tried for making offensive remarks about the doge and the Council of Ten. Instead of the four-month prison sentence handed down, at his own request, and armed at his own expense, he was allowed to serve the time in Albania fighting the Turks.

THE ALDINE PRESS AND VENETIAN PRINTING

TOWARDS THE END OF THE FIFTEENTH CENTURY the Venetians decided to grasp the new commercial opportunities opened up by book publishing. With its characteristic dynamism, Venice succeeded in establishing itself as an intellectual capital. Publishing and culture developed side by side, combined in the person of Aldo Manuzio who, having come from Rome, in 1495 set himself up in business at the sign of the Dolphin and Anchor – the fifteenth-century equivalent of a publisher's logo. His publishing masterpiece was undoubtedly the *Hypnerotomachia Poliphili*, a work of fantasy by the Dominican monk Francesco Colonna, written in a curious mixture of Latin and Italian.

At the end of the 1400s there were already a hundred and fifty printing presses in Venice – three times as many as in Paris, the other European centre of book production. Roughly a third of all the world's printed books at that time – two million in all – came from Venice. They covered a vast range of subjects, including medicine, law, politics, war, astronomy, time, the art of dying, the classics, education, religion, love and pleasure, all adorned with splendid illustrations. The artistic styles chosen ranged from the classical severity of the 1493 Italian Bible to the illustrations for Boccaccio's *Decameron*, which were full of narrative verve and sly humour. Taken as a whole, the imaginative quality and vitality of these illustrated works inspired major artists from Botticelli to Rubens and Veronese.

In the sixteenth century, as exploration continued apace, travel literature became particularly important. It built upon an earlier tradition, notably Marco Polo's *Livre des Merveilles* (Book of Wonders), followed by works such as *Paesi Nuovamente Ritrovati et Novo Mondo* (Recently Discovered Lands and the New World) by the Florentine Amerigo Vespucci and an anonymous 1490 edition of the *Portolano* which was attributed to Alvise da Mosto. The account of the first journey around the world by Antonio Pigafetta, a companion of the Portuguese navigator Ferdinand Magellan, who 'discovered' the Pacific Ocean, was published in Venice in 1536. The world had grown larger in the history books as well.

The current war against this age-old enemy, under way since 1462, was going badly for Venice. On mainland Greece the Turks had attacked the Venetian base of Negropont (Euboea) with a fleet and ground troops; it fell in 1470 after almost three centuries of Venetian rule. During fruitless negotiations, bands of marauding Turks rampaged throughout the Friuli region.

Cyprus was a strategic stronghold in otherwise Turkish waters that the Venetians were anxious not to let fall into the wrong hands. In the early 1470s, on the sudden death of James of Lusignan, King of Cyprus, who had married a Venetian noblewoman, Caterina Cornaro (also known as Corner), a coup was staged with the intention of handing over the succession to a bastard son of King Ferdinand of Naples. The Venetians reacted at once, sending a fleet to gain control of the island and thus establishing indirect rule. Eventually Caterina handed over the island to the Venetians entirely and returned to Italy to receive the signoria of Asolo, where she kept a brilliant court.

During the 1470s the whole of the Dalmatian coast bordering on Albania, where the situation was deteriorating, was under attack from the Turks in the person of the Pasha of Romania, who was advancing with ten thousand men and some heavy artillery. In 1474 the Senate sent Alvise da Mosto on a diplomatic mission to local rulers on the eastern Adriatic, as well as ordering General Captain Pietro Mocenigo, the doge's nephew who was stationed in Albania, to prepare its defences – even though he was sick with malaria. The same order was sent to the captains of all Venetian vessels in the vicinity, while further reinforcements were sent from Venice.

When the invasion started, two strong forts were built at the entrance to the port of Cattaro to prevent the Turkish forces impeding Venetian ships coming to the aid of the besieged inland city of Scutari. Crossbowmen and other military assistance were also sent to Scutari, where Bernardino da Mosto was stationed, by boat across a lake. So the Turks abandoned the siege and turned their attention elsewhere: Drivasto, a village on the River Kiri northeast of Scutari, where Giacomo da Mosto was *podestà*. Under attack for six days, the village was eventually taken. The Turks dressed Giacomo in gold and sent him with other prisoners to stand beneath the walls of Scutari to convince the regiment there to surrender. Bernardino may not have recognized his relative dressed up in this fashion, and the gates of the city remained closed. The poor man was first impaled and then beheaded, while the other prisoners were all cut to pieces.

Another Giacomo da Mosto, *bailò* (ambassador with responsibility for economic affairs) in Corfu, was more fortunate. In 1479 he received a letter from a successor Mocenigo doge, Giovanni, informing him that peace had been made with the Turks. Alvise da Mosto received a similar message from the Senate, together with special instructions to behave with great circumspection towards the Turks until certain matters had been resolved, and to stay on his guard as if still at war. Given the Turks' barbarous ways, it was probably sound advice.

In 1480, the painter Gentile Bellini was sent to Constantinople as a sign of friendship to the Turks; he made a portrait of Sultan Mahomet II (see page 110) while, back in Venice, his brother Giovanni was painting the famous portrait of Doge Leonardo Loredan. Court painters notwithstanding, the Turks then attacked mainland Italy, landing at Otranto in the southeast. However, a Turkish internal crisis following the death of Mahomet II enabled Venice to recoup the rights, privileges and exemptions of the Venetian *bailò* in Constantinople.

GENTILE BELLINI AT THE COURT OF CONSTANTINOPLE

SINCE THE TURKISH SULTAN was Muslim and the Venetian doge Christian they should have been enemies, even on the rare occasions when they were not officially at war – but business has always been more important than religion in Venice. The Republic had traditionally been synonymous with politics and money, but art was becoming important too. Now that the two powers had signed a peace treaty, Sultan Mahomet II was moved to send a Jewish diplomat to Venice to request a talented painter, and at the same time invited the doge to travel to Constantinople to attend his son's wedding.

In 1480 the Senate despatched the distinguished Gentile Bellini, who found the sultan to be an erudite patron of the arts and founder of notable institutions. Gentile portrayed the customs of the Eastern peoples, his natural bent for drawing enabling him to represent scenes and figures with great accuracy. But even in a sophisticated and cultured court, some of the more distasteful aspects of Turkish *mores* were on display. Mahomet commissioned a painting of St John the Baptist's head on a platter, the saint being revered by the Turks as a prophet. When Bellini presented the completed work to the sultan he praised it highly but also

remarked that, despite the painter's reputation for shrewd observation, he had made the saint's neck protrude too far from his head. Gentile seemed surprised, so the sultan summoned a slave and had him decapitated to demonstrate that, when a head was separated from the torso, the neck shrank. No doubt the sultan had seen rather more headless bodies than Bellini. The painter, greatly alarmed, tried to resign, fearing the same fate if he fell into disfavour.

His fears, however, were groundless. When Mahomet authorized Bellini's

departure he greatly praised his virtue and knighted him, placing a valuable gold chain around his neck. On his return to Venice, the Senate awarded Bellini a pension for life. Nevertheless, even though the artist had been returned home safely, an uneasy peace existed between the doge and the sultan. Fearing the worst, Venice prepared for war.

Above: Bellini's portrait of Sultan Mahomet II painted in 1480 while his brother Giovanni undertook a portrait of the sultan's opposite number in Venice, Doge Leonardo Loredan.

At about the same time Pope Sixtus IV, who was seeking Venetian help in fighting the king of Naples, awarded the Republic a free hand against Ferrara. Some of the Venetian troops were under the command of the brothers Andrea and Natale da Mosto, who were both wounded in battle. But Venice's successes in the Po valley region were greater than anticipated, and perturbed Sixtus IV so greatly that he issued a papal interdict. Eventually, under the settlement of 1484, Venice was allowed to keep the territory it had gained.

Beyond mainland Italy in the *Stato da Mar*, discoveries such as the sea route to the Indies and the existence of the New World were pushing Venice's trading network to the verge of crisis. In Egypt spices suddenly became rare and expensive, while the prices on the European markets dropped spectacularly; galleys were making their way back to Venice with their holds half-empty. In addition, the overland caravans were now heavily taxed, and novel products, such as coffee and tobacco, were all the rage. But competing in these markets implied a clash with the major European powers.

At the end of the fifteenth century France and Spain, now powerful nation states, looked towards Italy as a territory to conquer. In the first few years of the new century there was a continual shifting of alliances and war fronts for both the *Stato da Mar* and the *Stato da Terra*.

Venice allied itself with the king of Naples, the Hapsburg emperor and Duke Sforza of Milan against King Charles VIII of France, who had brought an army into Italy to conquer the Kingdom of Naples. In 1495 they succeeded in halting him at Fornovo in Lombardy, although the Italian forces suffered huge losses and the French army was able to retreat northwards. This bloody battle represented a watershed in Italian history, the beginning of the crisis of the country's piecemeal swallowing up by foreign powers. It would not recover its independence for another three hundred and fifty years.

Venice then occupied the ports of Apulia in southern Italy, important strategic positions for the control of the southern Adriatic; but in 1499, when the Republic concluded a treaty with Louis XII of France, it found itself in conflict with Lodovico il Moro, Duke of Milan, who encouraged the Turks to renew hostilities against Venice. My forebear Domenico da Mosto, Count of Nona on the Dalmatian coast, sent an alarming report from there in March 1500: 'After the raid of the Turks 33 active men are missing, 1179 women and children, 1252 large animals and 630 small ones.' Within a few months the situation had deteriorated further. A force of some four thousand Turks approached Nona; a small party managed to knock down the walls and force entry, but were driven back. The next morning the Turks attacked again, but still unsuccessfully; even the women

PROSTITUTES AND COURTESANS

VENICE WAS EFFICIENT IN ALL MATTERS. Sixteenth-century tourists in the city could consult a directory of ladies of the night and discover their names, their protectors, their place of residence and reception, and how much a gentleman would have to pay for their services.

Indeed, the oldest profession had been regulated for some two hundred years. In 1360 the government ordered the leaders of the six *sestieri* to find a location at the Rialto in which to concentrate the brothels. A suitable group of houses was found and it came to be known as the Castelletto because this medieval red light district was heavily guarded and it was governed by strict rules which were more suited to a fortress. The premises, supervised by six custodians, were closed every evening when the third bell of St Mark's had finished ringing and on all the main religious holidays. The girls had to obey the *matron*, whose job it was to collect all their earnings and divide them up at the end of each month. Although they were forbidden to move beyond the confines of the Castelletto, the women repeatedly flouted the law and were punished for so doing. An ancestor of mine, Piero da Mosto, leader of his *sestiere*, was attacked and fatally wounded by a group of

resentful noblemen while he was taking some prostitutes to prison. The residents of the Castelletto later dispersed to other areas, including the quarter known as Carampane.

Once the vice of sodomy began to spread in the city in the eighteenth century, the Republic actively encouraged prostitutes to flaunt themselves in doorways and windows, with lanterns lighting their wares in the evening. To entice the men away from 'unnatural sins' they would lounge bare-breasted on their

balconies. This is the origin of the Ponte delle Tette, which marks the boundary of the Carampane.

Living quarters were not the only restrictions placed on prostitutes. They could not own a house on the Grand Canal; nor could they travel along it during peak hours, or float through the city in two-oared boats; they could not enter churches on solemn occasions, or wear 'white maidens' veils' or cloaks; they were not supposed to adorn themselves with gold, jewels or pearls, whether real or paste, and were obliged to wear yellow scarves as a mark of their trade. Neither they nor their pimps could give evidence in court, and they could not go to law to exact any payments due. In exchange for relative tolerance, the dues they paid to the Senate were enough to maintain a dozen galleys.

As in most societies with a highly developed sense of pleasure, Venice also possessed genuine courtesans, including the famous Veronica

Above: Relief over the entrance to the San Domenico hostel, which was founded by Doge Marino Zorzi in 1312 as a home for fallen women. Opposite: A detail from a painting of 1490 by Carpaccio, commonly thought to show courtesans bleaching their hair in the sun. However, recent revelations suggest that these are fine Venetian ladies awaiting the return of their men from hunting on the lagoon.

Franco. Born around 1546 into a rich family, she established the image of the courtesan for centuries to come: beautiful, cultivated, unscrupulous and adventurous. Veronica combined the commercialization of sex with cultural refinement, and many of her own literary compositions were praised by writers of the day. She also frequently hosted concerts which were conducted from the harpsichord by the famous organist of St Mark's, Girolamo Parabosco. Immortalized by Tintoretto in a beautiful portrait, Veronica was famous abroad too, and many foreign poets dedicated verses to her. She loved the company of such men, to whom she would grant her favours in exchange for the opportunity to attend literary events at which she could join in the talk about poetry, art, philosophy or religion.

In 1580 she decided to change her ways, and with the help of some patricians – probably some of her former clients – she founded the *Casa del Soccorso* (House of Assistance) to provide shelter for women who wished to redeem themselves or who could no longer bear the life of prostitution. This institution gave them the material and spiritual comfort that only those who knew their world could offer; in this way the women could break free, either by taking religious vows, working in a family or by getting married.

and children fought – with sticks, as no money or ammunition had arrived. Apart from the failure of the supply line, local defences were poor, Domenico reported later: 'The Turks in the territory of Zara have captured three thousand people in a raid and the *proto* (chief architect) has built only half a tower, and without a parapet or battlements. A moat should be dug around the walls, ten paces wide and five or six feet deep, to prevent it from being forded.'

In February 1501, presenting the Collegio with a model for the defence of Nona, Domenico gave a report of a Turkish raid in which five people, including the vicar to the bishop, had wanted to surrender and had tried to persuade everyone else to do likewise. For this lack of fighting spirit he proposed that these five people should be sent to Venice 'in irons'. In the end, the city of Nona was saved almost miraculously. No more than two hundred people were left to defend the fortress, but the Turks retreated after their leader was killed.

The Venetian fleet, defeated by the Turks in the naval battle of Zonchio, lost many of the fortresses of the Morea in southern Greece. With its navy undermined by indiscipline and lack of experience among both the ordinary seamen and commanders, and with most of its resources being engaged on the mainland, Venice was forced to yield up part of its maritime power. The terms of the peace agreement of 1503 included the relinquishing of the bases of Lepanto, Modone and Corone, and the Republic's retreat was so ignominiously headlong that the sultan contemptuously claimed the right to wed the sea himself.

Although this was the situation overseas, back home the Venetians could take comfort from the legendary beauty of their women. On solemn occasions, such as the coronation of a dogaressa, a great procession of patrician women would make its way from the Piazza to the Basilica and the Doge's Palace, all dressed in satin, damask, velvet and taffeta, carrying gold-handled white feather fans and wearing gold bracelets and small golden crowns. A visiting fifteenth-century empress declared of the spectacle: 'I always believed the beauty of Venus to be a fable, but now I realize I was wrong, with all the Venuses I have met in this sea.' In a book of 1542 on the beauty of women, Nicolò Franco of Benevento describes the radiant beauty of the Venetians. He specifically mentions Marina Morosini, Maria Veniera and Marina da Mosto, '*la magnifica*', 'a great and profound image of beauty, of elegance, of gentility and of desire'.

Sansovino recounts that women wore multi-coloured robes, but, after the Greek fashion, covered them in black to contrast with their pale skins. This was the origin of the *zendado*, a light drape of black silk attached to the head. Their undergarments were richly embroidered and, to enhance their beauty, they would spend long hours on the rooftop terraces known

Opposite and overleaf: Two distinctive sections of the Grand Canal, without a doubt one of the most beautiful streets in the world. Venice's serene pace of life is reflected by the speed of the traffic on this, the main thoroughfare of the city.

as *altane*, wearing wide-brimmed but crownless hats to enable the sun to bleach their hair.

When Henry III of France visited Venice in 1574 a great ball was given in his honour in the richly decorated Sala del Maggior Consiglio. Two hundred noblewomen attended, all dressed in glowing white silk, with their breasts, necks, shoulders and hair adorned with jewels and pearls of great value. The French were so struck by their beauty that they asked the king's permission to remove their black cloaks, signs of mourning for his recently deceased brother Charles, so that they might dance with them.

It has been said that nothing reveals the nature of a society so clearly as the moral character of its women, who are never free and capricious if the men are not first dissolute. The Venetians managed to preserve their ancient modesty, and the austerity of their customs lay behind an old wives' tale in which the famous water of the Abano springs scalded women who longed to bathe where the men dived. But times were changing, bringing depravity with them, and the theatres and circuses were showing things they would once have blushed to hear mentioned. And, of course, some beautiful women were always willing to offer their services for payment (see pages 112–13).

THE LEAGUE OF CAMBRAI

On the mainland, meanwhile, other European states were on the move. More trouble was in store for Venice, as a formidable coalition was formed specifically to deal with the Serenissima: the League of Cambrai. War was declared in the year 1508.

After gaining control of the coasts of Le Marche and Puglia, Venice glimpsed a possibility for further mainland expansion in Romagna, which it hoped to snatch from the pope's control. But Venetian power in Italy, then at its height, had aroused a great deal of hostility: the pope, the emperor, the kings of Spain, France and Hungary were among those against Venice. They put their forces together to destroy the Republic, each one planning to grab a fistful of Venetian territory and wealth for itself.

Although Venice had levied an army superior in all senses to that of its opponents, France and the imperial troops nonetheless proved victorious in their first offensive at Agnadello, occupying Venetian mainland territory. Venice saved the day by using political acumen. The Apulian ports were given up so that an agreement could be reached with Spain, and the Republic managed to placate Pope Julius II, who realized that the ruin of Venice would be more dangerous than its power. On the mainland the peasants had risen up and retaken Padua, defending it against the imperial forces.

But the cards were shuffled once again and all the alliances switched: this time it was the pope and Spain against France, with Venice joining France and reconquering Brescia and Verona. At the end of seven years of ruinous war Venice's mainland dominion was re-established as far as the River Adda in the Lombardy region, which remained the Venetian border until the end of the Republic.

The war waged by the League of Cambrai brought to a halt Venice's plans for expansion; after gaining control of the Adriatic coast, it was constrained to shrink back within its former borders. Had Venetian dominion been more extensive, Italy would have gained politically, economically and socially. As it was, after the war Italy became more bitterly divided, poorer and weaker.

Even though the cities on the mainland had been sacked, the countryside devastated, the coffers drained and trade reduced to a mere trickle, the image of the Venetian Republic had maintained its lustre: with much of Europe united in opposition, Venice had held out. The Republic was now widely admired. Few could fail to respect a city that had been independent for so long and that managed to remain so with all the odds stacked against it. Venice's capacity to resist amid the general tragedy of Italy's lost freedom guaranteed the preservation of its role, despite everything, as a major power.

After the crisis, expansionist aims were shelved and the city entered a phase of neutrality; but, thanks to the immense capital the Republic had accumulated during its golden age, the slide into decadence was slowed down and there were even moments when it seemed poised for recovery. The city, which had been enriched by nine centuries of trade and war, was like a necklace of precious stones, continually enhanced and embellished. Philippe de Commines, a French diplomat, had been sent to Venice in 1495 to prepare the Italian expedition during the negotiations that preceded the Battle of Fornovo. He subsequently wrote an account of his journey in which he declared:

> *They took me along the main street, which they call Grand Canal and it is truly broad. Galleys travel along it, and I have seen ships of four hundred tonnes at anchor by the houses. It is, I think, the fairest street in the world, with the finest buildings, and it goes all the way through the city. The palaces are very large and tall, in good stone … It is the most triumphant city I have ever seen, the one that pays the greatest honours to ambassadors and foreigners, the city that is most wisely governed and in which God is most solemnly celebrated. And while there may be other faults, I think that God protects them for the reverence they show towards the Church.*

By the second half of the fifteenth century, the layout of the city, scarcely changed today, had been firmly defined in terms of the network of the canals, *calli* (streets) and *campi* (squares). St Mark's Basilica and the Doge's Palace, its most important public buildings, were largely complete.

In the buildings of Venice marble was employed not in great blocks but in thin sheets, reflecting the light of the sky and the water. In the paintings of Giovanni Bellini proportions, colour and light express a new dimension formed by water and sky, with the façades duplicated in the shifting, oscillating reflections in the canals. And in the pictorial imagination of Carpaccio and the architecture of Mauro Codussi, space is measured by light, through the qualities of colour. Examples can be found in church façades, where the half-circle of the *lunetta* window suggests an ideal horizon, and in palaces of carefully calculated proportions, with dark spaces between the luminous columns and delicately modulated reliefs like the folds of a veil. Since the lagoon and fleet gave sufficient protection, Venice had no need for intimidating defensive structures.

During the course of the fifteenth century, Venetian architecture had undergone a change in its relationship with European and Eastern styles. A delightful example of Eastern influence can be found in Pietro Lombardo's church of the Madonna dei Miracoli, with its delicate geometrical patterns of inlaid marble, which point to Byzantine origins. The sculptural works of Antonio Rizzo (for example, the Giants' Staircase in the Doge's Palace), on the other hand, suggest northern European influences whose contours have been softened by an encounter with the art of Giovanni Bellini, showing a sensitivity to the luminous and atmospheric qualities of the setting.

In synthesis, the old Venetian Gothic style was confronted by the new classical style. Beyond the obvious observation that classical has columns and rounded arches while Gothic has pointed arches, these two styles had more profound differences. The classical style was seen as clean, intellectual and mathematical, based on the architecture of Ancient Greece and Rome, but was at the same time new and different; whereas many saw Gothic as old, confused and unstructured – yet this was the style that dominated. The merging of the two created a whole new system of shapes to be used in architecture, making Venetian buildings seem truly unique. One fateful night in 1514 the opportunity to rebuild the city was presented in the most terrifying way: Venice burned.

Opposite: The church of the Madonna dei Miracoli is an elegant and imaginative Renaissance jewelbox of precious marblework, reputedly made from materials left over from work on St Mark's Basilica.

3

AIR

THE SERENISSIMA EVAPORATES

In the mid-sixteenth century, when that amazing new delicacy the potato had arrived in Europe, and when England had left the Church of Rome while Michelangelo was completing its great focus, St Peter's, Venice found itself caught between the Turks and the Hapsburgs of Austria and Spain. All it could do, after the power struggle in Italy between France and Spain had been won by the latter, was prepare to defend itself by any means possible.

While in Toledo, Gasparo Contarini, Venetian ambassador to the Hapsburg Emperor Charles V, had met the navigator Sebastiano Caboto and learned of his plans to explore ocean routes to the New World. Contarini put this idea to the Venetian government.

The project offered enormous commercial opportunities, but to reach these new markets they would have to embark on a massive conversion of the Arsenale and reorganize Venice's entire trading network. It would mean building ocean-going ships, such as galleons or caravels, rather than traditional Venetian galleys. And Venice would have to revolutionize its foreign policies, giving up its privileged relations with the East, and enter into open conflict with Spanish and Portuguese interests.

Venice's and Spain's interests against the Turks coincided – to a degree. Venetian naval expertise could be of use to Spain, but not to the point of reinforcing Venice's position in the Eastern Mediterranean, which would also have made it stronger in Italy.

Opposite: The church of San Giorgio Maggiore at dawn.

OTHELLO: BLACK AFRICAN OR DARK ITALIAN?

VENICE, the cultural and commercial gateway between East and West, was a place where for hundreds of years many races and religions let mutual economic benefit override differences. The 'Moor', a term to describe Muslims of black African origin, had been part of Venetian culture since the twelfth century.

In *Othello*, the story of a jealous husband incited by an embittered colleague to suspect his wife of infidelity and then murder her, Shakespeare used his imagination to reconstruct the Venetian setting, well known in England because of commercial and political connections. It was, perhaps, with knowledge of Giovanni Sanudo's brutal murder of his wife Lucrezia Cappello, word of

which had travelled surprisingly far, that he had Othello ask Desdemona, before killing her, if she had said her prayers to reconcile herself with God.

Associations have also been made with the figure of a captain, possibly an African mercenary in Venetian service, who had killed his wife in

Cyprus out of jealousy and was sent to Venice for trial. But who was Othello really? My grandfather Andrea, director of the Venice Archives in the 1930s, discovered him to be a southern Italian, Francesco da Sessa, known as *il Moro* or *capitano moro*, possibly because of his dark skin. In 1544 he was sent in chains from Cyprus to Venice, where he was imprisoned by the Council of Ten. At his trial the charge was uncertain, the verdict not unanimous, and no one could agree the punishment. In the end he was banished from the Republic for ten years, contravention of which would result in life imprisonment. Considering the uncertainty of the judges and the lightness of the sentence, his crime may well have been one of passion.

Above: A statue of Ser Antonio Rioba, a 'Moor' who fled from Morea (Greece) with his two brothers, Sandi and Afani. Opposite: Tintoretto's shop, also adorned with a statue of a 'Moor'.

Charles V had been defeated by the Turks at Prevesa in 1540, and in the subsequent treaty Venice lost bases in the Morea. Two Venetian statesmen had betrayed the Republic, and neither was the current state of the Venetian navy entirely satisfactory. Its galleys were crewed by free sailors enlisted for wages, including a great number of Dalmatians, Cretans and Greeks, but these were insufficient and Venice, like other naval powers, was now forced to use convict oarsmen chained to the benches. There are those who claim that in this time of *condottieri*, mercenaries and galley slaves a 'Moor' was taken on as a captain by the Republic, and that he was called Othello. But the details of the tragic tale taken up by Shakespeare and Verdi remain shrouded in mystery (see above).

At this dicey political moment, when Venice felt menaced by the Hapsburgs on the mainland and feared new betrayals, the government of the Serenissima established new organs of control, such as the State Inquisitors, subsequently known as the Supreme Tribunal. There were three – one, known as 'the red', selected from the ducal councillors who wore

scarlet robes, and two from the Council of Ten, known as 'the blacks' for the same reason. Created as a security unit, they gradually took on some of the powers of the Ten and made use of a network of anonymous informers for espionage, counter-espionage and internal surveillance. There was a saying in those days: 'In prison with the Ten, below ground with the Three.'

In the city there was a great blossoming of Renaissance arts. New palaces were embellished with beautiful paintings, and marvellous sculptures were created, such as the large statues of Neptune and Mars on the staircase of the Doge's Palace known as the *Scala dei Giganti* (the Giants' Staircase). Some Venetians, such as Marcantonio da Mosto (under the pseudonym Nicolò Liburnio), translated Greek and Latin writers. But other members of my family were engaged in more traditional pursuits. Two da Mostos, both called Giacomo, were grappling with life at sea. The first, captain of a galley of convicts, was awarded 200 ducats for good service and the care he had taken of his crew, of whom a mere fifty-two had died in four years – the life expectancy of a galley slave was brutally short. The second crushed raids by corsairs in 1568 and two years later steered his ship against the Turks. He surrendered at the Cypriot stronghold of Famagusta, where the Turks submitted the Venetian commander, Marcantonio Bragadin, to monstrous torture and humiliation and then skinned him alive.

Below: Jacopo Sansovino's figures of Mars and Neptune preside over the Giants' Staircase in the Doge's Palace, designed by Antonio Rizzi. Opposite: Andrea Palladio designed much of the monastery of San Giorgio Maggiore, but this double staircase is by Longhena. Pages 128–9: The church of San Giorgio Maggiore – one of Palladio's most important sacred buildings.

VENICE RESURGENT: A PHOENIX FROM THE ASHES

IN 1514 VENICE BURNED for twenty-four hours and all of the Rialto, the commercial hotbed, was destroyed. It was a tragedy, but also a great opportunity to rebuild. The Republic was losing its power, and needed to feel at least psychologically solid, lasting and impervious. A choice between Gothic or classical styles of architecture was made. They went for classical, giving Venicea a sense of order and security.

Inspired by the grand architecture of Ancient Rome, the classical was simultaneously old and new in Venice, and it made the place feel like another Eternal City. Jacopo Sansovino, whose work was classical, but sympathetic to the old Venetian style, quickly found favour. In 1529 he was made superintendent of works for St Mark's Square and the Doge's Palace.

The building of the Library of St Mark's dominated Sansovino's life, both imprisoning and bankrupting him, but in the end it was a triumph. Classical elements abound: obelisks, keystone heads, spandrel figures and a rich frieze with garland-bearing *putti*, framed by Doric and Ionic capitals. Sansovino's training as a sculptor is revealed by the ornate façade. This building in particular managed to equate sixteenth-century Venice with the power of Ancient Rome.

Carried away with visions of the ancient world, Sansovino had almost forgotten that he was building on water – and in 1545 disaster struck when a bay of the library collapsed. The furious authorities jailed him like a common criminal, despite his claim that the cause was gunfire from a nearby ship, together with frost. On his release, the architect was made to pay for the damage and rebuild the library at his own expense. It took him twenty-five years to pay off the debt, and he died before seeing the building finished, but he left a body of work that marked the start of an architectural revolution and changed the way Venice looked for ever.

By the 1560s Venice was becoming a truly Renaissance city – white, grand and elegant. Andrea Palladio, a quiet, intellectual scholar of ancient architecture, had become known for his magnificent, classical villas and palaces on the mainland. His innovative plans for building in Venice were continually rejected, mostly in favour of Sansovino's. Venice's affluent, conservative establishment resisted his pioneering ideas as long as possible until eventually he was asked to design just the façade of the church of San Francesco della Vigna – the rest was by Sansovino.

In contrast with Sansovino's penchant for deep sculptural surfaces, Palladio's gift was for creating simple yet imposing edifices. He took everything Sansovino had done and made it bigger and bolder. His ecclesiastical buildings reflected the theatrical character of the city, like sets on the largest and most elegant stage in the world. The monastery and church of San Giorgio Maggiore provided a fantastic extension to the triumphal surroundings of St Mark's Square. This was Palladio's first building in Venice and perhaps his greatest. With its unprecedented huge columns and triangular porticos, it shocked and astonished the Venetians. Inside, he expressed his love of circular ancient temples by making the church's shape radiate from a huge dome placed exactly at its centre.

A coalition was now set up with Spain and the pope as the major partners, along with Venice, Genoa and the Maltese Knights of St John. This so-called Holy League made it possible for a large fleet of two hundred and eight galleys, roughly equal in number to that of the Turks, to assemble under the command of King Philip II of Spain's step-brother, Don John of Austria. Over a hundred of these vessels were Venetian, commanded by Sebastiano Venier. The other great Venetian contribution to this naval enterprise was the provision of six huge galleasses. These state-of-the-art fighting machines, the pièce de résistance of the sixteenth-century Arsenale, were the big battle-cruisers of their day. The shape of this more sophisticated development of the galley enabled galleasses to be armed with heavy cannon in the bow as well as on both sides. Their disadvantage was lack of manoeuvrability, which meant they had to be towed into position by traditional galleys.

The Turkish fleet had sailed up the Adriatic and then returned to Lepanto (modern Navpaktos) in the Gulf of Patras to take on supplies, while the Christian fleet was concentrated at Messina in Sicily. They met in the waters of Lepanto on 17 October 1571 to fight a battle that altered the course of history – not because the Holy League's victory considerably weakened the Turks but because it was interpreted then, by both Christians and Muslims, as proof that Europe could halt the expansion of the Ottoman Empire into the Mediterranean. What could have been an isolated episode in the centuries-old conflict between Islam and Christianity became the start of a revival of Christian military opposition to the Turks.

As was customary in naval warfare at that time the Turkish admiral, the Sultan Ali Pasha himself, had positioned his ships in a long line divided into three squadrons. The Christian admirals had done the same with the papal, Venetian and Spanish galleys along an opposing front. To the Turks the small flotilla of accompanying galleasses seemed like huge, clumsy supply barges; but the Venetians knew they could deliver 'shock and awe'. Towards midday, from an advanced position, they began a devastating bombardment of the Turkish fleet. In just thirty minutes, ten thousand Muslim sailors and dozens of galleys were put out of action. Exploiting the enemy's disorientation, the Christian forces moved in for the kill and boarded a large number of ships including that of the sultan. In the assaults on the decks the Christians had the better of the poorly equipped archers and footsoldiers of the Turkish infantry. Ali Pasha himself was beheaded. It was the technological superiority of the Christians – equipped with better heavy artillery, with armour and arquebuses, and organized with iron discipline – that gained them the upper hand.

News of the victory caused great joy all over Europe, especially in Italy and Spain, although the allies did not fully exploit their tactical advantage and made separate peace agreements with the Turks. Venice had

Previous pages: Both the monastery cloister and church interior of San Giorgio Maggiore illustrate Palladio's exceptional talent. His ideas were innovative and shocked and impressed the Venetians. Even today, the stark elegance of his geometrical compositions may seem avant-garde.

proved it was still an important naval power, but its control on the trade routes was diminishing and it had gained no strategic advantage. Cyprus remained lost to the Turks, and Philip of Spain was too concerned with the western end of the Mediterranean and with Africa to want the Christian fleet deployed in the East.

A DEATH SENTENCE ON THE SERENISSIMA

In the summer of 1575 the city was sweltering under a pall of heat and humidity. Then, suddenly, the canals began to swarm not only with gondolas but with anxious rumours: 'A man died after a few hours of raging fever – then two, then a whole family.' And a terrible word rang out between the *campielli* and *calli*, the equivalent of a death sentence on the entire city: 'Plague!' It had already struck other parts of Europe, but this time it had not been halted, as sometimes in the past, on the edge of the lagoon.

People of all classes and ranks – the epidemic made no distinction – died after terrible suffering. Gondolas were now used for funerals, and cargo boats were full of corpses. The canals filled with the unburied bodies of poor wretches who fell sick and collapsed into the water, so finding at least a quicker death. In this apocalyptic scenario, the government did not know what to do.

A huge range of preventatives and cures was suggested, from sincere religious, philosophical, moral and medical theories through to ideas based purely on speculation and profit. An act of God, the influence of the planets and stars, climate change and air pollution were all mooted as possible causes. Western culture at that time was most influenced by the Arab doctrine that considered astrological events to lie at the root of famines, earthquakes and plagues, to be countered only by supernatural events, such as miracles or by demons.

Along with its valued goods, Venetian trade brought constant risk of infection, which could spread from ships' crews to the population. Nor were such epidemics restricted to bubonic plague: smallpox, typhoid, dysentery, whooping cough and cholera could all slip ashore from the *fondamente* and cause huge loss of life. Such outbreaks were dealt with not only by the Magistrato alle Acque, which supervised the circulation of water in the lagoon based on the ebb and flow of the tides, but also by the Provveditori di Comun – the Venetian public-health inspectors. The latter controlled the freshness of food, such as fish, meat, poultry, vegetables and cheese, together with the cleanliness of the city, ensuring that waste water was channelled into the canals and that livestock were not allowed to pollute the freshwater cisterns.

To prevent disease arriving from abroad, regular health bulletins were

THE GOLDEN AGE OF VENETIAN PAINTING

SOME OF VENICE'S most talented artists were working during this period, embellishing both the old city and the new one that grew up after the great fire. Titian, born sometime in the 1480s or 1490s, took Venetian painting to a new level of beauty, sensuality and eroticism. He trained under Gentile and Giovanni Bellini; mythologies, allegories and religious paintings in his distinctive style flowed from his studio. Unequalled in his rich and sensual use of colour, he took the realistic brushstroke of the Renaissance artists and gave it a softer and more expressive edge, and his use of light seemed to bring his figures to life. More than any other portraits the world had seen, Titian's seemed real.

My own first encounter with Titian was the painting of the Assumption on the high altar of the church of Santa Maria Gloriosa dei Frari, an image that has always touched me deeply. To me, his painting did not stop at the physical image but went deeper to express its spiritual aspect. Brushstrokes of an almost Impressionistic type depict the face of God who, hidden behind a grey beard, looks with suffering and helplessness at the state of his children. It is almost as if the experiment of man, from the time of the Creation itself, had proved a disappointment.

As his fame grew, Titian entertained scholars, artists and many of Venice's loveliest women at his home-cum-studio. He learned about the ancient classical culture that influenced his choice of subject matter from the architect Sansovino and the poet Aretino. And from the women of Venice he discovered feminine beauty, the glorification of which would bring him great renown.

Titian was a Venetian and, as with all of us, trade was in his blood. He willingly took commissions from the rich and high-born. The Duke of Urbino asked for an image of Venus. For centuries the nude had been a favoured subject for artists, and the more realistic nudes of the Renaissance had become erotic icons; but there was always something chaste about the figures, who closed their eyes or turned away from the gaze of the viewer. In an earlier painting by Giorgione, Titian's teacher, the goddess of love touches herself – but her eyes are closed and she is in her own private world.

Above: A detail from Titian's *Assumption* in the church of Santa Maria Gloriosa dei Frari, showing the face of God looking down at his children.

requested from the Republic's ambassadors based in the places where traded goods originated, particularly Constantinople, so that they could if necessary be quarantined in Dalmatia or Istria. There was a permanent blockade at the Lido port entrance, where the documents and cargoes of incoming galleys were checked; all passengers had to have a health certificate. If an infected ship was found, the sick and their belongings were sent to the island of Lazzaretto Vecchio, while the healthy were quarantined on Lazzaretto Nuovo after being washed with vinegar. But in 1576 all this had evidently not been enough.

In June, a meeting was called in the hall of the Great Council in the presence of the doge to evaluate the nature and extent of the danger. Two

Titian's *Venus of Urbino* was different: she looked straight at the viewer.

As Venice turned its back on the Church, so did its artists. Veronese, one of many contemporary artists influenced by Titian, painted a Last Supper that incurred the wrath of the Vatican's secret police, the Inquisition. In the eyes of the Church the painting was blasphemous because it included 'buffoons, drunkards, Germans, dwarves and similar vulgarities'. Pragmatically, Veronese merely renamed his picture *Feast in the House of Levi*. Aretino defied the pope by publishing a set of pornographic prints that had already been banned by the Vatican, dedicating the images to those 'hypocrites [whose] bad judgement and damnable habits forbid the eyes what delights them most'.

Jacopo Robusti, the son of a *tintore* (cloth dyer), hence his assumed name 'Tintoretto', was born in Venice in 1518 and may have worked in Titian's studio. He was a hard worker, and the lamp in his rooms always burned late as he studied the fascinating effects of light and shade. Tintoretto was aware of his worth, and did not suffer fools. When a nobleman who wanted his portrait painted insisted on the importance of doing justice to his splendid clothes and jewels, the artist lost his patience and exclaimed: 'Go and get your portrait done by Bassan!' – a famous painter of animals.

In 1564 he started his major work of decorating the Scuola di San Rocco, one of the Confraternities of Artisans, for an annual fee of 100 ducats. He worked there, on and off, for more than twenty years. Tintoretto had been chosen for this as the result of a competition, for which, contrary to the rules, he had painted his trial piece directly on to the ceiling (thanks to the complicity of the caretaker) instead of submitting a mere sketch. Naturally, he won.

Many Venetian artists were also musical: Tintoretto played various instruments and even invented some new ones. His friend, the enigmatic Giorgione, also enjoyed music but had a very different lifestyle. Tintoretto was a committed family man, whereas Giorgione suffered from what we would nowadays call sex addiction and died young of venereal disease.

Tintoretto's creative impetus never flagged: at the age of almost seventy, assisted by his son and followers, he conceived and painted the colossal *Paradise* for the hall of the Great Council in the Doge's Palace. The artist worked on his final masterpiece, the *Last Supper* for the church of San Giorgio Maggiore, right up to his death.

distinguished professors from Padua went round the city by gondola accompanied by two Jesuits and some barber-surgeons. After visiting infected houses, where they felt the pulses of the sick, lanced their buboes and bled them, the 'experts' blamed the outbreak on malnutrition in the lower classes and publicly proclaimed that there was no risk to Venice as a whole. Unfortunately, though perhaps not surprisingly, one of the Jesuits later died of the plague and his colleague and a barber-surgeon became critically ill with it.

The causes being unfathomable, the epidemic was attributed to collective punishment by the Creator: the patriarch gave weekly communion, using pincers more than a metre in length to keep his distance, and then,

after three days' fasting, visited the churches barefoot and dressed in sack-cloth, offering penitential psalms and pardons for sins. Pope Gregory XIII himself, fearing he would be accused as the instigator, revoked all the interdicts launched against the Republic.

Unlike most European states at this time, Venice had an excellent health system. The traditional doctor's plague mask with crystal eyes and a long beaked nose stuffed with perfumes was now a thing of the past and had been replaced by gloves and a cane. The cane was intended to prevent passers-by from coming too near to a doctor who had visited plague victims – sometimes little warning bells were attached to it – and it was also used to lift sufferers' clothes and bedding.

The treatment adopted for plague consisted of correcting the 'humours' (blood, phlegm, choler, melancholy) by way of bleeding or purging, while symptoms such as pustules had cupping glasses, poultices or leeches applied to them to draw out the poison. The first crude attempt at vaccination was made by the medical examiner for the Lazzaretti: 'Dry the carbuncles attached to the body in the sun, then make these into powder and, mixing it with half a spoonful of bugloss and endive water, take it in the morning on an empty stomach, then wait four hours before eating.' But despite the serious efforts made by official doctors, their helplessness in the face of the visitation of 1576 destroyed faith in them and desperate people put their trust in profiteers and charlatans. Many Venetians relied on the famous elixir known as *teriaca*.

The treatment of suspect furniture and household possessions had its own protocols: one entrepreneur applied to the Senate for a concession to process the contents of the sheds at the Lazzaretti. The contract made him responsible for cleansing the infected items, which were placed for five days in wooden crates filled with salt water. To avoid speculation, a detailed price list was drawn up that took into account the type and value of the objects to be disinfected.

One major problem in preventing the spread of the epidemic was finding corpse-carriers who would take away the bodies and burn them or bury them in common graves: 'one layer of bodies, one of quicklime and one of dirt', to destroy the disease. The Senate had tried to enlist people, but the pay was not enough to outweigh the risk of death. Efforts were made to enlist those under the death-sentence, which included a certain Francesco Mantovano. Condemned for blasphemy, his sentence was repealed for the service, but inevitably he was to pay with his life for that unexpected freedom.

The Senate refused to be intimidated by the epidemic and continued to meet. When only three hundred of the Great Council's thirteen hundred members presented themselves, the rest having fled to their villas on the

Opposite: Venice has been the inspiration of and home to fabulous works of art. The Sala del Maggior Consiglio in the Doge's Palace has a ceiling painting by Veronese representing the apotheosis of Venice crowned by victory, and below, Tintoretto's vision of *Paradise* is a feast for the eyes.
Overleaf: The plague epidemic of 1575 spread quickly among the narrow canals of Venice.

Below: The ghostly island of Lazzaretto Vechio, inhabited only by stray dogs today. Plague victims who died here could see the city that was their home, knowing they would never return.

THE LAZZARETTI: HAUNTED ISLANDS OF THE LAGOON

THE PLAGUE WAS A FINANCIAL DISASTER TOO. Ships and goods arriving from the East had to be kept in quarantine, their goods crammed into the warehouses on the islands of Lazzaretto Nuovo and Lazzaretto Vecchio. A church dedicated to Santa Maria di Nazareth was on the latter, from which the name derives; *lazzaretto* was taken up all over the world to mean quarantine station. These islands in the lagoon still seem haunted by the desolate atmosphere of those terrible days: moaning and wailing, foul air and burning bodies, the sick lying in agony three or four to a bed, eventually to be tossed on to the ever-growing pile of corpses.

Ships arriving from countries affected by plague were kept under observation on Lazzaretto Nuovo, then 'purged and fumigated three times with pitch'. Venetian citizens suspected of infection were housed here and given free treatment. When the hundred rooms on the island were full, old galleys and boats moored nearby provided accommodation. Detainees struck by disease were moved to Lazzaretto Vecchio; those who stayed healthy were sent home after twenty-two days.

Francesco Sansovino, son of the architect, who witnessed the events of 1576 and lost his eleven-year-old daughter Aurora, described Lazzaretto Nuovo as a symbol of the perfection of Venetian government:

The land of plenty, a floating city with more than three thousand boats anchored, is a place of enjoyable and cheerful appearance where a wonderful harmony of different voices rang, which at the sound of the Ave Maria praised God, singing litanies or psalms, and greeting the new arrivals with happy applause. The only jarring note was under the flag marking the impassable boundary – the gallows erected for those not obeying the orders of the Provveditori alla Sanità [public-health officials].

A dramatic description, quite the opposite of Sansovino's, was written by a sensitive and understanding notary, Rocco Benedetti, of the place that is now a home only for stray dogs:

The Lazzaretto Vecchio resembled hell, with an unbearable fetid stench emanating from all sides; you could hear the constant groaning and sighing and at all hours see clouds of smoke rising into the air from the burning of the bodies. Some tell how they got out alive by a miracle and how, enraged by the disease, they jumped out of bed at night and went running and screaming like the damned; some rushed furiously from the rooms and threw themselves into the water or ran to the gardens where they were found the next day bloodied among the thorns. The Lazzaretto Nuovo resembled purgatory where the unfortunate suffered from the death of their relatives, bemoaning their miserable state and the desolation of their homes; eight thousand invalids languished in the Lazzaretto Vecchio at the height of the plague.

TERIACA, THE GREAT PANACEA

———

IGNORANCE, TRICKERY AND SUGGESTION helped to keep this bizarre potion going at a time when medicine and quackery were indistinguishable. *Teriaca*, a Venetian speciality, was a blend of hundreds of ingredients from the commonplace to the arcane. Recommended for all sicknesses, even though completely ineffective, it must have had some psychological value (and hence financial worth) since it moved the authorities to threaten dire penalties for its falsification. The elaborate composition of this remedy, the search for the most exotic and expensive ingredients and the magnificent public ceremonies that surrounded its preparation became a State enterprise.

Into the mix went rose essence, gentian root, aniseed, cinnamon, squill, rhubarb, rosemary, pepper, a rare root from Zanzibar, centaurea from Asia Minor, terebinth from Cyprus, dittany from Crete and opobalsamum, a resin sold for a king's ransom extracted from a plant that grew only in Egypt and was said to be protected round the clock by armed guards. Added to this already rich and exotic *mélange* were snake flesh and the hearts and livers of deer, wild boar, eagles and ravens. Before consuming a meal where poison was suspected – after all, everybody who was anybody in Venice had enemies –

one was advised to knock back some *teriaca* as a prophylactic.

By the sixteenth century, the making of *teriaca* had become a piece of public theatre played by strict ceremonial rules, as described by the spice seller Giorgio Melichio in 1595: the ingredients, kept in precious silver bowls, were first displayed for at least three days in front of the 'authorized' pharmacies where they were guarded like gold. Before the weighing ceremony 'a black silk cap was given to the chief, the assistant chief and the pharmacy workers; that of the chief was decorated with three plumes, two red and one black; that of the assistant chief with two plumes, one red and one black, and those of the workers with one red plume'. The workers who ground the ingredients in a mortar wore 'a yellow woollen cap with red drawstring and red plume', and those who weighed the ingredients were offered 'a refreshment with lemon water, chocolate and sponge cake'. The result was then presented to His Excellency the Cassier (the cashier) in a silver glove box for safekeeping. Finally, the preparation was sealed in special jars to be opened two months later before the heads of the Spice College.

These rituals were so lavish that at the end of the eighteenth century the cost of preparing the medicine outweighed that of the ingredients. Mass-produced and exported, *teriaca* became a major source of income for the Venetian Republic. Possibly no other Western medicine survived as long as *teriaca* – and perhaps never will.

mainland, it decreed that at least one person from each noble household should carry out the functions of the *deputato di sestiere* (head of the sanitary police) – enormous fines would be levied on absentees.

The city's population was reduced by 25 per cent by the plague, whose victims included the great artist Titian and his son. A record was kept of all deaths: each house concerned was immediately sealed up and its inhabitants confined for up to forty days before the building was fumigated with sulphur, myrrh and pitch. The experience gained by Venice saved it from other epidemics, and the preventative apparatus of the Provveditori alla Sanità was to be used as a model by the most powerful states of Europe right up to the late eighteenth century. But more centuries were to pass before it was understood that rats and their fleas were the carriers of the bacillus.

By the end of 1576, when the epidemic had run its course, there had been fifty thousand victims. Where ordinary citizens had put their faith in quackery, the Venetian nobles put theirs in the clemency of God. In December that year the Senate decreed that a church dedicated to the Saviour Redeemer of the city should be built. A few months later a temporary altar was set up where Andrea Palladio was to erect the church of Il Redentore, a grandiose ex-voto temple.

Opposite: A seventeenth-century pharmacy in Canareggio that is still open for business today. Below: A gigantic cruise-ship towers over Venice. In the foreground is the *Dogana* (customs house), which originally controlled who and what entered the city.

IL REDENTORE: A TEMPLE OF THANKSGIVING

IN THE POST-PLAGUE CLIMATE of religious fervour a great church was to be built on Giudecca. At its inauguration a bridge of eighty galleys, flying the banners of the Serenissima, was put together across the Giudecca Canal, with cloth-covered arcades extending to St Mark's. Doge Sebastiano Venier crossed the bridge at the head of a solemn procession to the temporary altar. This ceremony has since been re-enacted annually – although in 1610 the bridge broke and dozens of people ended up in the water.

The first stone of Palladio's church of *Il Redentore* (the Redeemer) was laid in 1578 and it took five years to complete. Although the Signoria had decreed that 'there should be no marble, but it should be a strong building and one befitting a consecrated church', the Capuchin monks, whose site it was, were 'appalled by the magnificence of the building, almost as if denying the poverty of St Francis', and asked that the choir be built according to their rules. Palladio concurred, but even so the eventual cost of the building was at least twenty times the original estimate.

The façade is enriched with niches and columns, and bears a cornice and frieze in terracotta, rather than the unacceptable marble. There are also terracotta elements inside which are coloured to resemble stone.

The church is topped by an impressive dome the same width as the flight of steps outside, which recall the entrance to the Temple of Jerusalem and an episode from the Bible in which King David halted a flood that was threatening to engulf the city.

Nowadays, the evening of the annual pilgrimage on the third Saturday of July, is one of the highlights of the Venetian calendar of festivities. Music resounds across the lagoon, lanterns adorn the boats, filling the waters between St Mark's and the island of Giudecca, and the sky blazes with fireworks. The food, strictly seasonal and traditionally Venetian, includes fish *saor*. This dialect word means 'flavour', and the dish was invented in days when there was a lot of fish but little means of keeping it fresh. Preparing it in a well-flavoured marinade overcame this problem and preserved the fish for several days. Here is my father's recipe, a piece of Venetian social history:

According to a popular Venetian saying, the types of fish used for the saor *indicated the different social classes, associating them all in a dish. Sardines, the most popular fish, were the food of the poor,* passarini *[small lagoon sole] that of tradesmen and the well-off, and superior sole that of the nobility.*

The fish are scaled, their insides and heads removed and, after washing, they are coated with flour

and fried in a pan full of oil. They
are then drained and salted. Lots of
sliced white onions are then put into
the same oil and fried until golden,
then vinegar is added, keeping it on
the heat until it evaporates. The fried
sardines and the onion-and-vinegar
mixture are arranged in alternate
layers in a deep dish. This is kept
in a cool place for a couple of days,
then the saor is eaten with roasted
or cold polenta. Sultanas and pine
nuts are also often added to the
various layers.

If your mouth is already watering,
here is what you need for four
servings: 650 g (1 lb 7 oz) sardines,
800 g (1 lb 12 oz) white onions,
200 ml (7 fl oz) oil, a wineglass of
wine vinegar (not malt vinegar), some
plain flour, salt, and an optional 50 g
(2 oz) each of sultanas and pine nuts.
These last two ingredients, which
point to Eastern influences on
Venetian cooking, should be lightly
browned in the pan before being
added to the dish. Buon appetito!

Opposite: Palladio's Il Redentore.
The towers on either side and the
cupola recall the minarets and domes
of the East.
Above and right: Venice's fish market
is as vibrant as it ever was.

Above: The twenty-four hour clock in the Campo San Giacometto, close to the Rialto, where Venice's first banks were set up. It is still a bustling area with market stalls and the comings and goings of the nearby courtrooms.
Opposite: Drawings of the decoration on the Ca' da Mosto (1852) from John Ruskin's sketchbook.

ANOTHER REVIVAL, ANOTHER INTERDICT

The plague might have brought Venice and the economy of the Republic to its knees, but afterwards a new vitality was unleashed in individuals and in the community as a whole. Only ten years later, in 1587, the Venetian government set up the first public bank, the Banco della Piazza. After the sensational collapse of one of the private banks this was followed by a second public bank, the Banco Giro. These institutions were very important in financing the Serenissima's forthcoming wars with the Turks (as ever), Austria and the Balkan Uskoks, as well as conflict over Valtellina on the Swiss border and for the succession of Mantua and Monferrato.

The Banco Giro was where credit was born and where paper replaced gold. The first-ever bank loans were issued here. The Rialto had long been the banking centre of Venice, and Venice's banks were way ahead of their time. This had been the financial centre of the world, the Wall Street of its day, as far back as the twelfth century. The first banks in Venice appeared in the 1150s and were privately run, mostly the businesses of noblemen. The first government-controlled bank was, in the main, the safe custodian of deposits. Rather than issue notes payable, it administered the transfer of holdings from one name to another and rendered deposits to customers whenever they needed them. The bank was closed an extraordinary four times a year for drawing up its balances and transferring assets to the State mint. This consisted of a procession along the Mercerie when all shopholders stood guard in their doorways, armed and ready to defend the treasure.

In the city, while many sumptuous new palaces were now being built, the Ca' da Mosto went out of my family's possession when one of its members died without heirs (see opposite). At this time, too, the Rialto Bridge was constructed. On the mainland the first stone of the fortress of Palmanova was laid on the twenty-second anniversary of the Battle of Lepanto. Built in the form of a nine-pointed star, it was intended to reinforce the eastern border of the *Stato da Terra* against Turkish incursions into the Friuli and the expansionist aims of the Hapsburgs.

But this was not the only front on which Venice had to contend. Disagreements between the Republic and the papacy began with the election of Doge Leonardo Donà. Two priests were arrested for common crimes, and a law was passed limiting the acquisition and use of property by the Church. Pope Paul V considered these actions contrary to canonical law and asked for them to be revoked. When his request was refused he imposed an interdict prohibiting Venetian priests from celebrating religious offices, and excommunicated the city's rulers. Only a few years earlier he had told a Venetian ambassador that he had no hesitations about excommunicating Venice. The dry response he received was that in that event there would be

LOSS OF THE CA' DA MOSTO

THIS IS THE STORY of a da Mosto who married four times, had no children, survived the 1576 plague and, in 1600, made a will entirely in favour of a remote nephew of her second husband who had died over fifty years earlier. It is certainly not an affair of state, but it is a tale tinged with mystery, not to mention gold.

In 1536, Chiara da Mosto, the daughter of a well-to-do-family, married Domenico da Mula, who died soon afterwards. She married Giulio Donà in 1550; meanwhile, her father Benedetto had made her chief beneficiary in his will. When father and husband died she married again, in 1558. By now she was a rich woman.

Her third husband, Gerolamo Marcello, helped her considerably in property disputes with her relatives. He appeared in court on her behalf to claim rights to the Ca' da Mosto ferry, a vital crossing service on the Grand Canal, in front of the Rialto markets. Francesco da Mosto, a distant cousin of Chiara's, had claimed it and he had removed the jetties. In court the judges recognized Chiara's claim and ordered Francesco to rebuild the jetties or be sent to jail. She must have been very strong-willed, because when she lost her third husband she carried on fighting alone to recover the family palace, the feudal estates

and buildings of Torre di Mosto, cash and farms.

In 1573 she married, for the fourth and final time, to Sebastiano Barbarigo. Her wealth continued to accrue: in addition to property, she owned twenty-four boats and paid taxes to fund the equipping of galleys. She survived this husband too, and in 1602, in her old age, gave lands to her friends. She no longer had any contact with her family and her health was failing.

Despite extensive searches made for Chiara's will, through which the Grand Canal palace and other family assets changed hands, nothing has surfaced. But from some papers of my grandfather's I have been able to draw certain conclusions about its presumed contents and to establish that it was drawn up on 27 May 1603 by a notary named Marino Renier. Chiara's second husband's nephew Leonardo Donà profited well from his distant relationship, reinforced over the years by giving administrative assistance to Chiara. 'She ordains that she be buried at Corpus Domini with her mother and father. She leaves the manor house and estates at Torre di Mosto to the Donà family.'

After receiving the da Mosto inheritance Leonardo built an imposing palace on the Fondamenta Nuove, bought a hat shop on the Rialto Bridge and restored the old da Mosto palace and ferry on the Grand Canal. Originally single-storeyed in Veneto-Byzantine style, it is today the oldest remaining palace on the Grand Canal. A second floor was added at the start of the sixteenth century, and a third in the nineteenth. Leonardo's most picturesque source of income was the concession for the ferry known as the traghetto da Mosto at the Rialto. The twenty or thirty gondoliers who operated it paid him rent, which he passed to his brother Niccolò's wife to help maintain her many children. Educated and well-travelled, in 1606 he reached the pinnacle of his achievements when he became a conscientious though not popular doge.

no hesitation in rejecting the papal excommunication – which is exactly what happened.

The Serenissima, basing its claims on the principle that no citizen was exempt from the powers of the ordinary judiciary, was supported by its appointed spokesman, the distinguished theologian Paolo Sarpi of the Servite order. This remarkable polymath had worked with Galileo on telescope design, and was experienced in the fields of anatomy and botany, as well as being a learned historian and an able linguist. He originated the Venetian proverb: 'I never tell lies, but nor the truth to everyone', reminiscent of certain politicians' propensity to be economical with the truth. Although Sarpi recognized the pope's infallibility in matters of faith, he did not consider it extended further, and on behalf of the Republic he wrote spirited replies to the Vatican's protests. These were held to be heretical by the pope. So while Sarpi was venerated in Venice, beyond its boundaries he was considered an Antichrist.

Following revocation of the papal interdict a year later, with a compromise mediated by the French, Venice was satisfied. But Sarpi's troubles continued. In 1607 he was stabbed by three would-be assassins – who, he suspected, were in the pay of Rome. 'I recognize the style,' he said, playing on the Latin *stilus* – a word meaning both 'style' and 'knife'.

In matters of foreign policy, at the turn of the seventeenth century Venice was still a leading naval and economic power and maintained an enviable diplomatic organization in the face of the giants who now surrounded it: the Turks, Spanish, French, Germans and English. Problems arose when the galley of Cristoforo Venier (who was from the same family as Doge Sebastiano) was captured by the Uskoks, Christian fugitives from Bosnia and Turkish Dalmatia, who had been enlisted by the Hapsburgs to defend their borders after the treaty between Venice and the Turks following Lepanto, and Venier himself was barbarically slaughtered. The Uskoks had been in Venice's pay in the previous century but were now engaged in piracy in the Adriatic, so the Republic also found itself involved in hostilities on land with their protector, the Austrian archduke. The Serenissima sent an army against Gradisca, held by the archduke, while it gave financial assistance to the Duke of Savoy to counter another Hapsburg threat, the presence of the Spanish army in Lombardy. The military operations on this eastern front were not conclusive, but the peace of 1617 included a commitment from the Hapsburgs to resolve the problem of the Uskoks, who were sent to the interior, far from the Adriatic.

At the same time, the Spanish viceroy of Naples tried to undermine Venetian control of the Gulf of Venice by sending a fleet to the Adriatic, but he was defeated in 1617 and retreated. Meanwhile, rumours of a plot had been circulating in Venice, and there was unrest among the polyglot

THE RIALTO BRIDGE AND A PACT WITH THE DEVIL

In the heart of the city, spanning the Grand Canal, the most important thoroughfare in Venice, the Rialto Bridge has always been a symbol of trade and business. Its probable first version was built around 1181 by Nicolò Barattieri, the famous Lombard engineer who had distinguished himself in 1172 by raising the two huge granite columns in the Piazzetta San Marco. It was originally a simple bridge of boats, joined by planks of wood and known as the Money Bridge after the toll ferry it replaced.

The bridge was rebuilt twice, in wood, but in 1444 it collapsed under an exuberant crowd watching a parade of boats carrying foreign dignitaries. A further wooden bridge was built, but wider, with shops at the sides and with a central section that could be raised to allow high-masted ships to pass through; its form can be seen in Carpaccio's painting *The Miracle of the Relic of the True Cross on the Rialto Bridge* (see page 37).

Various restorations and proposals for replacement were prepared by

leading architects, including Michelangelo, Palladio, Vignola and Sansovino, then the entire Rialto district was devastated by fire in 1514. Again, all the big names were invited to submit designs for a new bridge, but all were regarded by the authorities as too radical. It was eventually decided that this vital link, then the only bridge across the Grand Canal, should be built in the classical style with wide arches and triangular porticoes. Not until 1588 did work begin on the present Rialto Bridge, distinguished also by exceptional engineering skill. Built of stone, with a single arch and a span of over 28 metres (92 feet), it carries two rows of shops and was constructed under the supervision of Antonio or Giovanni Contino, known as da Ponte, who had already built the Bridge of Sighs connecting the Doge's Palace to the prisons, and would go on to build the palace where I live, one of the highest in the city.

Objectors interrupted the work on several occasions, and the arch caused immense problems that could, according to legend, only be overcome through a pact with the devil. Chunks of stone kept falling off in the night, so a keen foreman hid nearby to see what was happening. At midnight there was a loud cracking sound, then a splash as a huge section of the arch broke away. Cackling with laughter, the devil appeared and announced: 'No man will ever succeed in building this stone bridge, but for a price I can help you.' The trembling stonemason asked if he wanted his soul in return. 'No,' replied the devil. 'Just the soul of whoever crosses the completed bridge first.'

The Rialto Bridge was finally finished in 1591 and its splendour silenced even the most vociferous critics. At the inaugural ceremony a dog ran ahead of the priest who was about to climb the steps to bless the bridge, saving him and trapping the devil's soul as he fled. The structure was so solid that it was a hundred years before any restoration was required.

mercenaries enlisted for the war against Austria. It seemed that the Spanish ambassador was aware of the conspiracy. The Council of Ten, informed by a Huguenot captain, tracked down the perpetrators, who were punished. Three of the Venetian thugs known as *bravi* were hanged, and the Senate asked for the Spanish ambassador to be recalled. Despite this, the peace between Venice and Austria was ratified in Madrid in 1618.

It was a period when the *bravi* rampaged in Venice, and not even my own family remained unaffected. Domenico da Mosto was the black sheep of the time, known to consort with *bravi*. Arrested by the Council of Ten for killing a linen merchant, he was sentenced to permanent exile or ten years' imprisonment – which was, however, soon commuted to ten years' banishment on Corfu. The spirit of the times was contagious: a Francesco da Mosto was arrested after almost beating to death a merchant, his tenant, for having damaged a newly restored house. But a little mayhem and the occasional murder were mere trifles compared with what happened to one poor man at the hands of the State.

In 1622 Antonio Foscarini, a senator and ambassador to England, was accused of spying for a foreign power and of having revealed the Republic's political strategy to the Spanish Emperor, Ferdinand II. He was tried on the first count and acquitted, but condemned on the second and was subsequently hanged between the columns on the Piazzetta. A few months later, the Council of Ten discovered that the dead man was the innocent victim of a plot. The slanderers were condemned to death, and the rehabilitation of the victim was proclaimed with a circular to all European embassies: 'Divine Providence has ordained that this council should have well-founded and clear light on the wickedness of those who made unjust accusations and made the false appear true. So the pristine state of honour and reputation shall be attested and shown to be true by Public Decree.' But, alas, by then it was too late.

In the city, thanks to the family's excessive power, all four sons of Doge Giovanni Corner I held important public offices, even though one of them had actually committed murder. Some patrician families objected violently to this state of affairs, and to settle the discord the Council of Ten decided that in cases of state crimes or those involving patricians the Great Council too would have to deliberate.

Certain aspects of Venetian history are cyclic: after a great famine there was another outbreak of plague in 1630. In sixteen months a third of the population died – almost fifty thousand people, or ninety thousand including those on the lagoon islands. In thanks for the ending of the epidemic another church was planned, and the first stone of Santa Maria della Salute was laid by the winner of the design competition, Baldassare Longhena. The baroque style was in keeping with the prevailing secular tastes.

GRATUITOUS VIOLENCE: THE *BRAVI*

———

THE BULLYING AND ARROGANCE that were so prevalent in Venice from the late sixteenth century to the early eighteenth gave rise to the phenomenon of the vicious and amoral *bravi* – akin to mafia hit-men. These generations of Venetians were characterized by a sense of pride and independence; they were more likely to take justice into their own hands than to appeal to State powers, partly because such powers were generally inadequate. To bully the weak, or simply to stand up to the bullying of others, *bravi* could be recruited from among the delinquent youth of the time. They first emerged under Spanish rule, which encompassed most of Italy, and within the Papal States, but then spread to the rest of the peninsula.

Violence and harassment were mainly meted out by the higher social classes, but commoners would give them a helping hand. They hired themselves out as *bravi* and often behaved on their own account, just like the worst aristocrats, but perhaps with less publicity. Commoners could be seen at Easter picking straws to see who should kill the first person to pass by, or who should beat up the next person he came across – just for kicks.

The *bravi* of a certain Ser Vido Morosini responded to a poor wretch pleading to be spared by stabbing him twenty-seven times and shouting: 'This is the life!' Ser Agostino Lando demonstrated a typically cruel and rapacious mentality. Unable to get his hands on the belongings of one Nicolò Tagliaferro, due to the intervention of the Council of Ten, he had him killed and then, to frighten one of Tagliaferro's sons into signing a promissory note, he presented to him the *bravo* who had killed his father.

Bravi would use any means to achieve their ends. Bluffing was the most common method: they would treat an enemy like a friend, then stab him in the back. Ser Alvise Bon acted with astonishing coolness. Having discovered that his wife had become the mistress of his cousin Ser Andrea Trevisan, he went with her by carriage to meet Trevisan at his villa on the mainland. The three of them whiled away the hours with music and revelry, and Trevisan was so taken in by Bon's charm that he not only invited him to stay but even allowed himself to be found in bed with Bon's wife. This was precisely what the cuckolded husband wanted: with the assistance of a hired assassin he killed them both, stabbing the lover fifteen times and his wife thirty.

Often vendettas could be particularly ruthless and relentless. In 1608, in Verona, a soldier insulted a trumpeter, who vowed to take fearsome revenge. The soldier's apologies were rejected. A good three years later, the offended party surprised him in a *calle* and struck him thirteen blows with a sword, continuing to lay into his victim even after he was dead.

In order to reduce such violence in Venice, the Council of Ten moved to reconcile differences between noble families, summoning the contenders to appear before them. However, this often worsened the situation because on finding themselves face to face, these hot-headed men ended up fighting in front of the authorities.

The evil mind-set prevalent in this dark period could only be corrected by social change. Various Italian states exacted appropriate laws that gave the public legal protection, and at the end of the seventeenth century legislation against the *bravi* was brought into force in Venice. In January 1687, without regard for his own safety in the surrounding crowd, Capitan Grande Nicoletto da Ponte, the chief of police, arrested the much-feared *bravo* Francesco Giacomo Raspi under the Procuratie Nuove, where he daily traded the lives of men. He then sent Raspi's sword in homage to the Inquisitors.

The *bravi* disappeared from the Republic, but continued to be commissioned from time to time in Italian feudal territories. They were finally swept away at the end of the eighteenth century by the tide of the Napoleonic armies, who also phased out feudalism.

CRIMES AND PUNISHMENTS

CRIMINALS LOCKED IN THE STOCKS or hanging from the gallows could sometimes be seen between the two columns in the Piazzetta of St Mark's, delinquents were publicly flogged there and at the Rialto, and the corpses of the drowned were displayed for identification on the edge of the present Giardinetto Reale. Those condemned for the worst crimes were dragged behind a horse from Santa Croce to St Mark's before being hanged, although this was rare. Such spectacles would make us lose our appetite or at least our good humour, but our forefathers were less squeamish. Public executions eventually became infrequent – so much so that a foreigner who lived in Venice for six years saw the gallows raised on only one occasion.

However, these gruesome associations did nothing to prevent the upper classes from gathering every day in front of the two columns – in the morning under the portico of the Doge's Palace, and in the afternoon under the Procuratie Nuove. While the nobles were there it was prohibited to pass through the area they occupied. Elsewhere in the vicinity there were foreign merchants and idlers, who amused themselves watching the jugglers, the tooth-pullers and the fortune-tellers who spoke to the punters through long metal megaphones. Every now and then, at appointed hours, a town crier dressed in ceremonial costume would make public announcements in a stentorian voice. There was even a small stage where comedians would perform. And sometimes punishment and entertainment were mingled in a way that would not revolt even our modern sensibilities. A certain Alvise Beneto, who sent his wife out to work as a prostitute and carefully noted down the profits in a book, was sentenced to go round the city on a donkey, dressed in yellow and with enormous horns on his head.

Longhena also built the Ca' Pesaro (now the Modern Art Museum, with its impressive collection of Oriental decorative arts) and the Ca' Rezzonico (now the museum of the eighteenth century): their imposing façades on the Grand Canal develop the compositional schemes of Sansovino, whose works he had studied with great interest in his youth.

THE CITY AND ITS INHABITANTS IN THE SEVENTEENTH CENTURY

After the plague of 1630 the population fell to below 100,000, yet Venice was still the same enchanting temptress, able to attract great numbers of foreigners. Those who visited in this period characterized it as one of the grandest and richest cities in Europe, with more buildings than London – the number was much greater then than now, as Venice fell into decline in the nineteenth century when a lot of buildings were dismantled and the stone and decorations sold off. Many of the gardens that offered a welcome contrast to the density of the city also disappeared at that time. There were

---

Opposite: A narrow canal in the San Polo district opens out onto the Grand Canal – one of forty-five canals that feed into it.

NAUGHTY NUNS AND PASSIONATE PRIESTS

———

THERE WAS GREAT RELIGIOUS TOLERANCE in Venice, where the activities of the Inquisition were very restrained. The Catholic clergy were overseen by the patriarch, a Venetian nobleman who lived in a cloistered palace next to the cathedral of San Pietro di Castello. The ducal chapel of St Mark, however, was under the direction of the *primicerio*, a kind of nobleman-bishop employed by the doge. Church and State were kept firmly apart, and clergy were excluded from all government posts and offices.

Before 1600 Venice had thirty-odd monasteries and about the same number of convents – a total of some three thousand monks and nuns. They left something to be desired in terms of piety and behaviour. Priests and monks – and, it was rumoured, even cardinals – went, diguised behind masks, to theatres, parties and balls. One Neapolitan monk, also a professor at Padua University and a patrician legate, was said to have told the Bishop of Padua, who was trying to lead him back to the straight and narrow: 'My friend, if God has given you ice-cold passions, give him thanks. He gave me passions of fire and I don't know how to contain myself!'

Nuns created even greater scandal, especially those from noble families who had forced them to take vows – either because the family had more daughters than it could provide marriage dowries for, or because the woman in question had misbehaved with the opposite sex. They dressed their hair fashionably, wore low-backed dresses with bare arms, decorated themselves with flowers and used gloves, fans and jewellery. These 'nuns' would receive visitors in their luxurious parlours, behind iron grilles. At one point, to curb those of the San Lorenzo convent, all of whom were noble by birth, the Patriarch ordered them to stay in their cells in the afternoons, when unsupervised visits were usually made during siesta time. The indignant nuns climbed up to the roof and threw down oil-soaked rags that they had set alight: even the effigy of St Lawrence was burnt. The patriarch, wisely, let the matter drop.

During the Easter holiday of 1618, Piero da Mosto went out into the lagoon for a night-time picnic with two of his friends and his sister. They bought some fish from local fishermen and Piero's sister suggested they should go and visit their aunt, Sister Cherubina, in the convent of Sant' Anna and have the fish cooked there. As it was now some years since they had last visited her, they sent a servant ahead to announce them, and gave him the bucket of fish to present as a gift. Sister Cherubina insisted that they all come ashore, but Piero's sister refused because she was poorly dressed and was wearing unsightly shoes. They therefore decided to picnic further along the canal in a spot beside the convent cellars. Sister Cherubina brought two other cousins with her, Sister Nicolosa dei Foscarini and Sister Costantina degli Zorzi, and they made up a nice group of hearty revellers. But the improvised party was all too soon interrupted, probably even before the fish had been cooked, when they were seen by a magistrate's officer and Piero was subsequently tried 'for a rather too entertaining visit to his aunt'.

more churches and convents in the 1600s, too, many being demolished later after the fall of the Republic. Almost all the houses were built of stone, with very few remaining in wood. There were street names, though these were not written on the walls as they are today. Provisional numbers were given to the houses only when censuses were taken for application of the *decime* (property taxes).

The *calli, rughe* and *campi* – respectively Venice's narrow alleys, streets with shops, and squares usually outside churches – and the *fondamente* that ran alongside the canals were paved mainly with bricks laid herringbone fashion (as can still be seen in some out-of-the-way parts of the city) or with big white stone slabs. The *calli* were raised in the middle and sloped down at the sides, where gutters collected the water and drained it off into the canals. The bridges had no side rails and were narrower than now, with high steps in white Istrian stone that made them very dangerous when they were wet with rain or slippery with ice. A few wooden bridges still existed then, as they do now. The *fondamente* were also less wide than now, with an edging of Istrian stone, and people frequently slipped into the water.

Standards of cleanliness in the streets left a lot to be desired. Each district had street-sweepers who pushed the rubbish into special masonry enclosures, which were then emptied by boats known as *scoazzere*. Passers-by did not hesitate to relieve themselves in the streets: signs stating, *Chi qua piscierà, a casa del diavolo anderà* (Those who piss here will go to the devil) were often found on walls near churches. The canals also gave off a terrible stink, especially during lengthy wars when there was no money available for dredging, and the accumulation of mud and sand also made navigation difficult.

The dead, as in most places, were commonly buried in and around the churches. But Venice is not most places, being built on piles in a lagoon. It may have been a source of emotional support for people to live close to their departed loved ones, but hygienically it was most undesirable. Even today, in front of the churches of Sant' Angelo, San Beneto and San Trovaso raised ground can be seen, in which plague victims may have been laid. During outbreaks of plague, the stench of putrefying corpses from the often imperfectly sealed graves was appalling – not even incense could mask it. After the epidemic of 1630 a new floor was laid on top of the existing paving stones and tombs in the church of San Simeone Grande to suppress the emanations from those buried there.

The locals shrewdly observed that when walking around Venice it was wise to avoid three 'Ps': *pietra bianca* (slippery white stone), *puttane* (prostitutes) and *preti* (priests). Some added a fourth to these: *pantaloni* (figures of fun who represented the nobility). Members of this echelon of Venetian society considered themselves superior to other Italian and foreign nobles, and on a par only with princes. It is said that one of their number, when in Paris, declared that he was no less than the king's brother because any nobleman in Venice could become doge. The private incomes of the Venetian nobility were certainly equal to, if not higher than, those of their counterparts in other European countries.

The nobility were all equal before the law of the Republic, but used

Previous page: Narrow alleyways with uneven paving permeate the heart of Venice. This is the school of San Giovanni Evangelista. The wing above the column pictured here was my first school and I later returned when it became the University of Architecture.

to divide themselves into four ranks according to the antiquity of their origins. The first rank consisted of the so-called 'old' families, whose ennoblement dated from before the year 800. The second comprised 'new' families, which had been included after that date. Sixteen of these, known as *ducali*, devised a scheme to exclude the old families from the dogeship, and succeeded for almost two centuries. The latter, in retaliation, managed to exclude the *ducali* from the better-paid ducal appointments. The third rank consisted of the 'very new' families, ennobled in respect of financial and personal services provided during the 1380 war with Chioggia. The fourth and final rank consisted of families inscribed in the famous Golden Book during the war of Candia in the mid-seventeenth century and the war of the Morea at the beginning of the eighteenth. Their 'entrance fee' was the enormous sum of 100,000 ducats, and they were commonly known as 'nobles by payment'. In addition, the families of popes, sovereigns and other worthy citizens of the Republic could be made honorary nobles – though it happened rarely.

Above: The cemetery island of San Michele, which will be my last home.

The four ranks in total numbered about six thousand men, women and children. For the Venetian census the nobility was divided into rich, average and poor. The last of these were assisted with special grants and were known as the *barnabotti* because they lived mostly in the San Barnaba area where the rents were lower. They were the so-called commoners of the Great Council, made restless and unruly by their wretched condition.

Noblemen officially had the right to the title of *nobiluomo ser* (noble sir); whereas that of *eccellenza* (excellency), misused by many in later years, was reserved for certain important positions and that of *messer* (master) was given only to the procurators of St Mark. Various nobles had the personal title of *cavaliere*, obtained in the embassies of foreign sovereigns or because they were recipients of the knighthood of St Mark; it was a hereditary title in a few families only.

From the age of twenty-five, noblemen wore a black cloak and a round cap when outdoors, while underneath they sported the fashions of the day influenced by French tailoring. The young dressed richly in black beneath cloaks decorated with gold, silver or silk lace, and wore high-heeled boots. Knights were distinguished by a gold-threaded stole; the red ones of the ducal councillors stood out in the crowd of black-robed nobles, as did the violet ones of the chief magistrates and the purple ones of the procurators of St Mark. All the cloaks, apart from those of the Savi agli Ordini, had voluminous sleeves, giving rise to the term 'broad-sleeved' for ambitious and unscrupulous people. They all wore wigs during the second half of the seventeenth century, but when they were banned at one point, many nobles had to retreat out of the city to the country to grow back their hair, which had been shaved.

On ceremonial occasions, nobles wore a red robe. When they greeted one another, they doffed their cap with their left hand and put their right over their heart, and bows and curtseys were obligatory. The extravagant rituals portrayed in the comedies of the celebrated dramatist Carlo Goldoni are no exaggeration. A foreigner at the time wrote of having seen some officers from the Venetian army make obeisance at the entrance of a procurator of St Mark for a full quarter of an hour. People spoke and wrote with pompous circumlocutions. The nobility were called *illustrissimi* or *eccellentissimi*, the secretaries *clarissimi*, the citizens and nobles of the mainland *signoria illustrissima*, the merchants *vostra signoria* and tradesmen *signor*. Obsession with titles degenerated into farce, as a seventeenth-century poet observed: 'You citizens want to be addressed as *lustrissimo*; the merchant expects *clarissimo*; every scoundrel is *molto illustre* and the porters are entitled *magnifico signor.*'

One way of greeting a noble submissively was to kiss the sleeve of his robe, yet in order to obtain some favour even the most powerful nobles

Opposite: The unique shape of the Venetian gondola with its rich decoration. Black became the traditional colour when a sumptuary law was passed to limit extravagance.

'GONDOLA!'

IN SEVENTEENTH-CENTURY VENICE one had only to walk up to a canal and call: 'Gondola!' to be immediately attended to. In those days there were about ten thousand gondolas in operation. All had a *felze* (cabin) and were painted black on account of the sumptuary laws to prevent rivalry between noble families; the exceptions were those gondolas belonging to ambassadors and ministers residing in the Venetian Republic, which were gilded, gorgeously painted and carved. Gondolas then were differently shaped from today, and the *ferro*, the iron-work at the prow, was smaller. Functional as well as decorative – it gives balance to the craft – it was once known as the 'dolphin'. Its present form is said to represent the *corno ducale*, the doge's hat, with six forward-pointing prongs indicating the six *sestieri* (districts of the city) and one at the back for the island of Giudecca.

The gondola proved essential to Venetian life right from the start, allowing people to live on and move around the lagoon islands. Today it is still built in the city's *squeri* (boatyards) by a few survivors of dynasties who have handed down the secrets of the craft from father to son. Strict rules must be followed: the right half has to be narrower than the left for greater speed and to improve the turning circle; the length is fixed at 10.75 metres (just over 35 feet) and the internal width at 1.38 metres (4½ feet). Specific woods must be used for different parts of the boat, such as oak for the planking and larch for the bottom. It persists today as the ultimate expression of Venetian boat-building and testament to the marine engineering of the Serenissima.

could be seen bowing down before the poorest and least influential individuals. But clearly there was more to them than all this superficial show might suggest. A foreigner observed that the serious and pleasing physiognomy of the nobility showed intelligence, discretion and good nature, and even the least ostentatious seemed to him worthy of being sent as ambassadors to a European sovereign. He judged them loyal in friendship, and undaunted and unshakeable under the blows of misfortune – very different from the young layabouts of the eighteenth century who, as the war of the Morea raged, preferred to pay mercenaries to fight the Turks on their behalf.

In matters of religion the aristocracy were far from fanatical – 'Venetians first, then Christians' was their familiar watchword. It was said that a Jew who failed to remove his cap at the sound of the bells of St Mark's was given a slap to remind him by a passing nobleman. When the Jew humbly apologized, explaining that he was not a believer, the nobleman replied that he himself believed even less.

The nobles studied under tutors until the age of seventeen, when they entered society; very few went on to study at a university. But this limited education was compensated for by the natural instinct of the Venetians for affairs of state, and they reputedly took little interest in events elsewhere. The story is told of a nobleman who snatched a history of France from his son's hands, exclaiming: 'Blockhead – read things about your own republic and no other!' Not much importance was placed on moral education, as is indicated by the loose behaviour of the young that was tolerated by their families.

Like their fathers and husbands, aristocratic women dressed in the French fashion. They wore very low-cut dresses and the older women tended to deck themselves out just like the young, often making themselves look ridiculous. All ages went hatless, apart from unmarried girls, who wore large white veils. The girls were educated in convents, and when they reached marriageable age their family would select a suitable prospective husband.

A foreigner noted something odd about the physique of Venetian women: they were not very pretty without clothes because their legs were not straight, and they were pigeon-toed due to a ban on receiving dancing lessons. Or perhaps it was something to do with what they wore on their feet. Until the mid-seventeenth century, in order to avoid muddying themselves when negotiating the dirty *calli*, they wore *chopines*, tall clogs up to 60 centimetres (2 feet) high, which made the wearer fairly imposing. At home they needed extra-high chairs, and when they went for a walk they could only do so with the help of a maid.

Women were not supposed to wear jewels because sumptuary laws had been passed that forbade any display of wealth except on certain occasions. Only recently married women were allowed to adorn themselves – with pearl necklaces for two years. This was the case with women of noble birth, but there were also exceptions that confirmed the rule: the daughter of a gondolier, wife of a procurator, showed off her jewellery in order to efface the memory of her humble origins. And Venetian women, being fond of finery and full of ingenuity, soon found ways to evade the unpopular law.

The women lived in each other's company, away from the men unless closely related. Most of them led cloistered existences, appearing only for religious services, weddings and important festivals. But there were curious contradictions in their way of life. A minority of the upper-class women were notoriously extrovert and never missed a gathering. Ladies could dance with any guest at the major festivities where the uninvited and foreigners were allowed – provided they were masked. During carnival ladies often went out in masks, accompanied by maids, to public meeting places and to the theatre. Often good-looking and shapely, haughty and of slender but majestic stature (those clogs again), they were not allowed to speak so had to resort to gestures. One foreign visitor found these complicated and silent manoeuvres all too much for him; another, perhaps more fortunate, observed that in Venice you could make more progress with a glance than you could elsewhere with prolonged attention.

Where the patrician table was concerned, the nobles of modest means lived very simply on sardines, shellfish and whatever else was readily available; rich ones, on the other hand, were well provided with a wide range of fish and meat. However, the sumptuary laws restricted not only people's dress but also what they ate, decreeing that meat and fish should not appear at the same meal – it was not even permitted to ring a bell to announce that dinner was served. Nobles returning from the Paris embassy often brought French cooks back with them so that they could continue to eat the refined cuisine of that city. This was one area in which the Venetian countryside was better off than the city: a greater display of foods was accessible there to both rich and poor.

Below the nobles in the pecking order came the middle class, consisting of skilled craftsmen and professional men, such as accountants, law court officials, lawyers, doctors, surgeons, pharmacists, merchants, retailers of silk and gold cloth, and the glassmakers of Murano. There were about seven thousand of them, including women and children. The men could work in the State administration, as secretaries to the Council of Ten and the Senate, and as ministers in the secondary courts. Their leader was the grand chancellor, who enjoyed the title of *eccellenza*. They wore black cloaks like the nobles, but for ceremonies the secretaries wore violet. Their wives were treated as ladies, but of inferior rank to noblewomen.

The third social class was made up of commoners – dockyard workers, tradesmen, gondoliers and fishermen. The highest public office a commoner could aspire to was that of *capitan grande* – chief of police for the Council of Ten, the State Inquisitors and the Lords of the Night (the after-dark police force, as their name suggests). The *capitan grande* had a number of agents at his disposal, commonly known as *sbirri,* assisted by armed dockyard workers when required. There were a few paupers, but they were provided for by the State. Contemporary statistics show that there were two hundred or so beggars, plus thirteen hundred poor people cared for in hospitals.

The gondoliers constituted a very important section of the commoners. Those who were retained by the nobility were not so much servants as lower-ranking friends and confidants. So proud of their trade were they that, like their masters, they would sit in costume, surrounded by the banners they had won in regattas, for an artist to paint their portrait in oils. They were also literate and could recite the works of the famous poets Tasso and Ariosto. More than a handful of the two hundred-odd gondoliers working in Venice today are as cultured as their seventeenth-century ancestors.

As night fell, the city was shrouded in impenetrable gloom, dispelled only by the light of the moon, the soft shimmer of the stars and by the small oil lamps lit before sacred images in the *capitelli* (shrines), some of which can still be seen in various parts of the city, and by the beacons and lanterns of the passers-by. The *capitelli* were kept alight thanks to the piety of the locals and special charges enforced by public bodies, who entrusted their supervision to the parish priests. Venice relied on such lighting until the first half of the eighteenth century.

This was the Venice of the mid-1600s. The Serenissima was softer now, her magnificence slipping inexorably towards decadence, no longer the undisputed mistress of Mediterranean trade but still, alas, not yet finished with the Turks.

Opposite: The church of Santa Maria della Salute at sunset. On top of the customs house in the foreground sits a statue of Fortune, on top of a terrestrial sphere, that moves with the wind.

4

FIRE

VENICE BURNS ITS PAST

Between the 1620s and the 1640s the great scientist and thinker Galileo was put on trial by the Inquisition; in Britain, Charles I began to rule without Parliament, which would lead the country to a bloody civil war; and in the burgeoning New World the Confederation of New England was set up. In Venice the first public opera house opened in San Cassiano. Beyond the lagoon, however, there were more serious matters to contend with.

Fighting piracy in the Adriatic was a centuries-old Venetian right. In 1638 a Barbary pirate fleet made up of sixteen galleys from Algeria and Tunisia entered the Adriatic and was met by a Venetian squadron off Candia (the island of Crete), which the Venetians had purchased from King Boniface of Monferrat in the thirteenth century and colonized because of its strategic position on the trade routes. The Venetian ships followed the pirates to Valona, a Turkish stronghold, and shelled it heavily, capturing their galleys and freeing several thousand prisoners. Retaliating against the bombardment of Turkish territory, the Sultan arrested the Venetian *bailò* (ambassador with responsibility for economic affairs) of Constantinople, Alvise Contarini. While in prison, Contarini negotiated massive damages for the Turks. His advice to the Venetian Senate – perhaps still applicable in similar crises around the world today – demonstrated the Republic's typically pragmatic attitude: 'The cost of a month of war alone is the same as the sum paid, and a single year of traffic recovers it.'

The real war with the Turks began in 1644 following a raid on a Turkish convoy by Maltese pirates, who also captured part of the sultan's

Opposite: The Campanile of St Mark's, which was rebuilt in 1902 after it collapsed.

harem returning from Mecca. The pirates had stopped in Candia on their way home and the Turks used the Maltese action as an excuse to invade, as the position of the island made it a constant problem for their ships. Francesco Morosini arrived on the scene – a young, aggressive and courageous soldier who had been promoted to general at the tender age of thirty. Before the long drawn-out hostilities in the Peloponnese were over, he took on the roles of, first, villain of the piece and then hero, and he finally went down in history, alongside blind, aged Dandolo of Constantinople fame, as one of the great fighting doges of the Republic.

The bitter war in the seas of southern Greece continued for years. One by one the towns of Candia were taken by the Turks, until only Iráklion was left. But here the invaders were brought to a halt, and all they could do was besiege the town, but Venice somehow still managed to keep the place reasonably supplied – for an astonishing twenty years and more. Allies of the Venetians came and went, but by 1669 the garrison was so depleted that Morosini felt he had no option other than to surrender. A Venetian expression for a thin person, still in use today, recalls the sufferings of the starving inhabitants: *Seco incandio* (Dried up like a Candian). Surprisingly, there was none of the usual barbarity afterwards and the ragged survivors

Below: A detail of the symbolic relief work on Doge Morosini's barge. Opposite: One of the four lions that Doge Morosini brought back to Venice after his conquest of Athens, which now stand in front of the Arsenale.

were allowed to sail unmolested for home. On his return, Francesco Morosini was arrested and presented to the Venetian people as a traitor because he had surrendered without the Senate's permission. Although acquitted, he was ostracized. It was fifteen years before he could restore his honour, invading southern Greece at the head of a multinational force and taking more territory in the region than Venice had ever ruled before.

Morosini was undoubtedly a dashing and heroic figure, though this reputation is somewhat marred in the eyes of later generations. In 1687, during his invasion of the Peloponnese, he blew up a Turkish ammunition dump and the building in which it was housed: the Parthenon. After taking Athens he brought home the four lions that now adorn the entrance to the Arsenal, and for his great services he was honoured with the title *Peloponnesiaco*. In 1688 he became doge, while also retaining supreme command of the fleet. Pope Alexander VIII praised his efforts as a defender of the faith. But in the Aegean the war continued: more territory was lost, more money haemorrhaged from Venice's coffers. So in 1693, at the age of seventy-five, Morosini set sail to support the fleet in the hope of redeeming the situation. He took some islands on the Greek archipelago but then, exhausted by a life of war, died in Nauplia, in his own Peloponnese, where he had once been undisputed victor.

Da Mostos played their part, albeit marginally, in all these hostilities. A Lorenzo da Mosto was holed up in starving Candia during the siege while his wife back home in Venice gorged on vast quantities of meat, chicken and eggs. In their different ways they both suffered, however, for the lady in question was afflicted by a tapeworm. Lorenzo's relative Vettor II da Mosto fared rather worse – he was blown up with his ship during the invasion of the Peloponnese.

NEUTRALITY ABROAD, AMORALITY AT HOME

At the start of the eighteenth century the Venetian government chose 'armed neutrality' in preference to the hypothetical advantages offered by Austria and France, both of whom had produced claimants to the vacant Spanish throne in their interminable War of the Spanish Succession. The Serenissima was to make this its principal policy in the future, comforted in its inevitable decline by an atmosphere of exhilaration and by the enchantments of its courtesans, who attracted visitors from all over Europe.

Francesco Morosini's conquests in the Peloponnese did not last long. In 1714 Sultan Ahmed III declared war on the Republic and, since the Turks had already taken three of the islands anyway, the Venetian naval commander, Daniele Dolfin, thought it preferable to save his fleet rather than endanger it further. The Morea was left for the Turks. However, a

OLD FAMILIES DYING OUT

EVER SINCE I FIRST READ THE NAMES on my family tree, the da Mostos of the Vettor branch have always amazed me. In the mid-seventeenth century, before the long war of Candia, a branch of the family was started by a Vettor da Mosto. Either because he simply liked the name or because he was extremely self-centred or unimaginative, he called all his sons Vettor followed by a number. This practice continued with all his grand-sons and great-grandsons, until that particular branch died out.

Some see the decline of this branch as an example of how certain families started to die out near the end of the Republic, as if they had some premonition of imminent catastrophe. Around then there were more than twenty-five male offspring in one generation of my family, but in the next there was only one. A great black hole had swallowed up all hope for the future. Some nobles intentionally caused their houses to die by not registering marriages. Others, including two of the Vettors, remained bachelors.

After the first generation, most of the Vettors were commanders of ships, losing their lives in the wars against the Turks. In order not to risk the vagaries of chance, or perhaps as a kind of lucky charm, my wife and I called our first son Vettor. I had a feeling that, from the dim beyond, his eponymous forebears might supply him with some of their legendary energy; now that he is seven, I can testify that he certainly shows no lack of it.

Above: The da Mosto family in 2004. My grandfather risked letting the family line disappear into extinction, but then married when he was about 50 – now there are seven male members of the family. My oldest son, the latest bearer of the name Vettor, is seated in the front row, far right.

couple of years earlier the Venetians had managed to repel the Turks from Corfu, and for his part in the affair Vettor III da Mosto was awarded a gold medal. Meagre acquisitions were also made in Albania and Dalmatia, but after this no territories were won or lost by the Republic to the very end of its days.

This was no longer a military state. The Arsenale's slipways were launching not battleships but the last *Bucintoro*, the doge's gorgeous ceremonial barge. The city itself was protected only by two companies of *cappelletti*, Dalmatian and Albanian soldiers who wore a small red cap – hence the name. Armed with sabre and musket, they had the specific task of guarding the Doge's Palace and St Mark's Square. The lottery became a public institution after two hundred years as an unofficial affair, popular among the common people. Venice was crammed with sumptuous, well-stocked shops with characteristic painted, gilded or carved signs: certain *calli* must have looked like colourful forests. Amongst the pharmacies were *Al Salvatore* (Saviour) and *Alla Testa d'Oro* (Golden Head), while the shops rejoiced in such names as *Alla Novizza* (Newlywed), *Alla Bottiglia* (Bottle), *Al Melone* (Melon), *Alla Vite* (Vine), *Ai Due Profeti* (Two Prophets), *Al Paladino* (Champion), *Alla Gatta* (Cat), *Al Guerriero* (Warrior), *Al Cuore* (Heart), *All'Ancora* (Anchor) and *Ai Due Mori* (Two Moors), the last of which, still in existence, I visit regularly for an *ombra* of wine (see page 23) and a quick bite.

Perfumers, lemon sellers and water vendors had their shops under the old and new Procuratie where, from the end of the seventeenth century, there were also cafés. Some of the latter were off limits to Venetians unless they were nobles, but foreigners were always welcome, provided they did not belong to any of the legations – with whom the nobility were prohibited from having any contact. The Mercerie were full of shops selling silk, wool, gold cloth, gold and silver lace, ribbons, Damascus velvet and brocades at astronomical prices. Whenever processions took place, the shops were splendidly decorated and full of ladies watching the show. Campo San Bartolomeo, which leads from the Mercerie to the Rialto Bridge, housed some of the best grocers and shops selling goods from the Middle East and Germany; indeed, the *Fondaco dei Tedeschi* (German warehouse) still stands near by and is now the Post Office.

Crossing the Rialto Bridge, flanked as today with various kinds of shops, visitors would have come to the little square of San Giacometto with

Left: A bas relief on the exterior of the church of Santa Maria del Giglio showing the fortified town of Candia (Crete).

its porticoes full of goldsmiths and jewellers. Here, along with the pioneering banks, was a concentration of warehouses and all kinds of commercial offices, clothing and silk shops, the fish market, butchers and the fruit and vegetable markets: in short, the commercial heart and belly of Venice.

By now, however, the competition for trade had really begun to strangle the Republic. Goods sent to Lombardy, Germany and cities as far west on the Italian mainland as Verona were supplied directly by Venice's ancient rival on the west coast, Genoa, and by Genoa's neighbour Livorno (Leghorn), the port for English traffic in the Mediterranean. In the Adriatic goods from the Middle East, Albania, the other Turkish provinces and the West all arrived through papal Ancona and Hapsburg Trieste, where a free port had been established.

Even once the wars with Venice's trading rivals had all been fought and lost, the city still needed protection from the sea itself. In April 1744 the first stone of the Murazzi, designed by the Serenissima's cosmographer Coronelli, was laid. A solid wall of Istrian stone, 14 metres (46 feet) wide and 4.5 metres (nearly 15 feet) above average sea level, it was designed to protect the littoral between Pellestrina and Chioggia. This was to be the last great public work carried out by the Venetian State, which had always assiduously invested money and expertise in protecting the lagoon system.

In most people's minds, however, the Venice of the eighteenth century is still associated rather less with feats of engineering and flood defences than with a man whose name has become synonymous with debauchery and libertine behaviour: Casanova. Born in 1725 to an actress mother who preferred an independent life free of the ties of a family, he was brought up by his maternal grandmother. At the age of eight young Giacomo had frequent nose-bleeds, so she took him to a sorceress in Murano, who cured him and possibly gave him a taste for her bizarre trade. Soon after he was sent to Padua to begin his education – in all senses: here he had his first affair, with the sister of his landlord. While studying law at Padua University he made a further conquest in the person of 'Bellino', a singer who passed herself off as a castrato. After unsuccessful attempts at a career first in the Church and then in the army, he began to pursue his real vocation: that of adventurer. Living off his wits, he travelled all over Europe, consorting with sovereigns and artists, philosophers and scientists.

Like all extraordinary men, in the course of his life he played many different roles: actor, manager of lotteries, priest, violinist and spy. In 1755 he was imprisoned in the Piombi, the lead-roofed attic cells of the Doge's Palace. Casanova had aroused too much talk, and the Tribunale della Serenissima had ordered one of its informers to follow him: he was suspected of being a card-sharp, an unbeliever, a pimp, a holder of

Opposite: Carnival time, both now and in the past, conjures up a picture of Venice as a city dedicted to pleasure and amusement.

VISITORS, CARNIVAL AND OTHER AMUSEMENTS

AT CARNIVAL TIME, between Christmas and Lent, Venice was – and still is – thronged with foreigners; in one year, towards the end of the seventeenth century, a good thirty thousand came to enjoy themselves, including seven reigning princes. In 2004, seventy thousand visitors assailed the city on the first Saturday of Carnival – although not a single reigning prince among them. Carnival helped to create the image of Venice as a city dedicated to pleasure. In actual fact, the Carnival started off as an attempt to control the impulses since the indulgent revelry was merely conceded for a limited period. In the strictly hierarchical Venetian society, it also gave the humble classes an illusion of becoming similar to the more powerful classes, albeit wearing a mask, and served to diminish social tensions.

The Carnival has its roots in many traditions, including the Greek Dionysian feasts celebrating the start of spring, when masks were used for symbolic representation, and the Ancient Roman feast of Saturnalia, when the usual order of the year was suspended: grudges and quarrels forgotten, wars interrupted or postponed. Businesses, courts, schools all closed. Rich and poor were equal, slaves were served by masters, children headed the family. Cross-dressing, masquerades and merriment of all kinds prevailed. During Carnival there were dances in closed rooms and the venues, where people danced to the violin or spinet and the women were

all masked, were marked by a lantern and green branches. A visitor compared these dances to markets where the beauty of the goods on offer inveigled one into buying even when one had had no intention of doing so. Carnival is mentioned so often in the plays of Carlo Goldoni that his work has become an important source of documentation.

As happens frequently when other aspects of the economy have decayed, in Venice the tourist trade and related service industries brought in welcome revenue. The inns where the visitors lodged offered scant comfort. There was no running water and only commodes, small washbasins and foot-baths were provided. Bedrooms were small and often shared, as were the beds themselves. Rooms were not numbered but named: the king's room, the emperor's, that of the angel, the sun and the moon. One foreigner observed that the wines were either too sour or too sweet

and were often watered down, and that the bread was as hard as rock. But perhaps he had better luck with the entertainment. Venice had always been famous for its courtesans, many of them on the fringes of noble and middle-class life. They went about the city with their breasts barely covered and a posy of flowers behind one ear, parading in such bright red and yellow dresses that they were said to resemble tulips. Some *calli* were so infested with women vying for business that it was difficult for a man to free himself without leaving his sleeve behind. The most fashionable wore *chopines* (tall clogs) like high-class ladies. They were allowed to frequent the *freschi* (the summer gondola races on the Grand Canal) and the opera, but with their faces concealed behind masks. All wanted to be known as 'women of love', and venereal disease was rife among them.

Young commoners with compliant mothers could easily be procured for money. The open-air, public dances on Sundays began with these girls, dressed in white and decked out in ribbons and lace, dancing the traditional *furlana* from the Friuli region. The most attractive ones could expect to be set up in an apartment, perhaps by a young noble, as a kept woman; this status enjoyed a degree of respect, and afterwards craftsmen often married them. It is said that it was possible to get a nice girl for 150 silver *scudi* in cash, plus 150 per year for maintenance.

undeclared goods, such as a barrel of salt, and generally licentious. Indeed, his lover at the time was a Venetian noble's daughter whom he shared with the French ambassador; the lady in question was actually a nun in a convent in Murano who had taken religious vows on impulse. The members of the *tribunale* were particularly concerned about certain strange objects found in Casanova's house that alluded to black magic and freemasonry. But despite the notorious Piombi prison's reputation for security, he managed to break out and remove himself from the clutches of the State.

After more than a year of imprisonment, as he was to recount in his memoirs, Casanova made his escape. Along with another prisoner, a monk called Balbi with whom he had managed to communicate by exchanging books marked with secret codes, he cut through some wooden planks one night to reach an attic floor and from there clambered up on to the roof:

We went across fifteen or sixteen of those lead roofing sheets and finally found ourselves on the highest part; I spread my legs and sat astride: Balbi did the same behind me. We turned our backs to the small island of San Giorgio Maggiore and in front appeared the many domes of St Mark, which is part of the Doge's Palace. It is the doge's chapel: no king in the world can boast of having anything like it.

Not finding a place to attach the rope with which to let ourselves down, we slid down the slope and, hanging from the guttering, managed to get into the rooms of the palace offices. On the desk of the chancellery I found a metal tool with which I forced a wooden door, quickly collected my things, put on the street clothes they had allowed me to take to the prison and opened the door without difficulty.

Casanova then showed himself at one of the windows, and passers-by who saw him thought he was a guest from the previous night's ball who had been locked inside by mistake. They told the porter, who went and opened up the door. 'I quickly went to the Porta della Carta,' Casanova recalled, 'which is the main entrance to the palace, and, without looking at anyone, which is the best way to avoid attention, I crossed the Piazzetta and immediately got into the first gondola I saw.' And from there, as fast as possible, he slipped across the border to the safety of France.

In Amsterdam he fell for the fifteen-year-old niece of a rich merchant, but when she made it clear that she would allow him to bed her only after marriage he moved swiftly on to Stuttgart – but then had to flee over a gambling matter, so travelled on to Russia, Poland, Spain and back to France. Despite poor relations with the Venetian government, his attachment to the

Serenissima was powerful and reveals itself in his story 'The Duel', prompted by an insult murmured behind his back in the dressing rooms of a Warsaw theatre: 'That Venetian idler would do himself a favour by leaving.' Without turning round, Casanova replied: 'A spineless Venetian will shortly send a courageous Pole to the other world.' 'Idler' he could live with, but to hear the word 'Venetian' uttered in contempt was too much to bear. In Paris Casanova supported the plan of the Marquise d'Urfé, the 'sublime mad-woman', an occultist and one of the richest women in Paris, to change sex, reincarnating herself as a newborn baby. He then met the young and captivating Marie Charpillon, who aroused his emotions so deeply that he was driven to the brink of suicide: 'It was in that fatal September of 1763 that I began to die and finished living. I was thirty-eight.'

After eighteen years of this existence he returned to Venice, where he was reduced to spying for the State Inquisitors on a monthly salary of 15 ducats, collecting information in the cafés, meeting places and theatres and writing letters and reports. After three months, his appointment was revoked. Casanova, anxious to please, continued to write reports, though given his lifestyle, there is a certain irony in their subject matter:

In San Moise, at the top of the fish market on the side leading to the Calle del Ridotto beside the Grand Canal, there is a place which is called the painters' academy. In this place the students of drawing meet to portray a nude man in various poses on some nights and on others a woman. This Monday a woman will be shown, whom various students will draw nude, as she will present herself.

Various young artists who are not even twelve or thirteen years of age are also admitted to this academy of the nude woman. In addition to them, many amateurs who are neither painters nor sketchers, but merely inquisitive, also attend the show.

Casanova ended his days in a castle in Bohemia, working as a librarian. Here, old and alone, far from the salons, courts and theatres that had seen him as both spectator and actor, he set about writing his memoirs, a lively fresco of hedonistic, licentious, pre-revolutionary, eighteenth-century society.

EUROPE KNOCKS ON VENICE'S DOOR

Opposite: Canaletto's *Canal Grande dal ponte di Rialto verso la Ca' Foscari* (The Grand Canal from the Rialto bridge looking towards the Ca' Foscari), painted around 1740.

The world was changing, and science and new technologies were the driving force. Benjamin Franklin invented the lightning conductor, and James Watt the steam engine, although such innovations may not have made headlines in the *avvisi* (weekly Venetian newsheets) that were at first hand-written, then printed. While other states – Britain, France, Portugal, the Netherlands, Spain – looked outwards to colonial expansion, Venetians, their

IN THE EIGHTEENTH CENTURY townscapes became a highly fashionable subject for Venetian artists. Some painted imaginary scenes known as *capricci*, while others produced *vedute*, views of real buildings depicted with an astounding degree of accuracy and detail. The latter were facilitated by a *camera obscura*, a box with a lens which casts an image of the object being viewed on to a sheet of paper, which could then be traced. Among the most talented exponents of *vedute* were Antonio Canal, called Canaletto, and Francesco Guardi.

Canaletto initially worked with his father in Rome as a scene painter, then decided to devote himself to *vedute*. His work, characterized by brilliant contrasts between light and shade and a meticulous attention to detail, includes depictions of monumental architecture, views of the less well-known corners of Venice, and landscapes of incredible professionalism and charm inspired by the city, the mainland and its rivers.

ARTISTS: *CAPRICCI*, *VEDUTE* AND FRESCOES

Canaletto's work was appreciated by visitors, particularly the English. The British Consul, Joseph Smith, a collector and dealer, commissioned six magnificent views of St Mark's Square. In 1746 Canaletto went to England, where he stayed for over nine years, painting views of London, the Thames and the English countryside to which he managed to transfer the bright serenity found in his Venetian works.

Guardi trained in the family workshop and he was particularly sensitive to landscape and its atmospheric values. Human figures were of minor importance to him but, when included, were depicted with tiny, delicate brushstrokes. His *vedute*, at first influenced by Canaletto's brightness and crispness, later became more individualistic as Guardi adopted a style executed with rapid, darting brushstrokes, creating visions of vibrant brilliance. He re-created better than any other artist the damp, opaque atmosphere of the lagoon, where water and sky mingle on the grey horizon.

Totally different from these views of sunlit buildings and sparkling water was the work of Guardi's brother-in-law Giambattista Tiepolo, who created breathtakingly beautiful frescoes on walls and ceilings. Praised by his contemporaries, he was in demand by sovereigns, princes and nobles from all over Europe. His radiant works peopled with allegorical figures glorified noble dynasties – but Tiepolo was also a consummate painter of skies, who could be said to have reinvented the heavenly vault. His art is almost literally celestial, his brushstrokes at varying times lyrical, sensual, imaginative, illusionist, theatrical, idyllic or elegiac.

maritime empire now all but gone, employed artists to paint their city in all the splendour of its decline.

The increasing attacks of privateers along the North African coast were obstructing what remained of Venice's trade, forcing merchants to keep their ships in port or to sail them in well-protected and therefore expensive convoys. Diplomatic initiatives undertaken in the 1760s in Algeria, Tunisia, Tripoli and Morocco were successful in that they led to agreements, but Venice was obliged to pay stiff annual indemnities. Either way, it was a costly business and ate into profits. Eventually military action against Tripoli was mooted, but for some reason Venice's demands were accepted before any blood was spilt. The number of Venetian ships plying these waters increased rapidly.

It seemed that violence was more likely to break out back home, where public administration abuses and legal reforms were still under heated discussion. An attempt was made to break the monopoly of power held by a few rich noblemen, redistributing it in favour of the numerous poor nobles; it failed, and Giorgio Pisani and Carlo Contarini, representing the less well-off party, were imprisoned. Agostino da Mosto too was in trouble with the authorities for what they regarded as speaking out of turn. A man with a strong sense of duty and devotion to the Republic, he was never slow to share his views on public affairs. Ten years later he was again accused of speaking too freely and once more found himself in the clutches of the State Inquisitors. But despite such attempts to regain control, the government was moving inexorably towards its demise.

And still Venice played. For those wishing to amuse themselves, it offered more than any other city in Europe. As well as the public festivities – regattas, boxing matches, bull races, Carnival, the Ascension Day fair with its wooden booths set up in St Mark's Square – there were also 'special' festivals for the elections of doges and for the initiation ceremonies of the procurators of St Mark, of ambassadors and prelates, and for visits by royalty. On all these occasions masks were worn, often under the traditional Venetian tricorn hat called the *bauto*. The riding school at Santi Giovanni e Paolo kept almost a hundred horses; splendid tournaments and equestrian games in costume were held. At the end of the seventeenth century a more grisly entertainment was added: the public dissection of corpses in the anatomical theatre at San Giacomo dall'Orio.

The numerous *ridotti* (clubs) hosted gambling and were well populated with card-sharps. The main *ridotto* near St Mark's was a kind of Monte Carlo and belonged to the Dandolo family. Open during Carnival, it had one large room and other smaller ones splendidly illuminated by candlelight and offering restaurant service. The games were played in complete silence, almost always with cash stakes and only rarely on mere promises; masks

Opposite, top: Behind masks all Venetians were equal, an intrigue that heightened the spirit of the Carnival.
Opposite, below: A view of Venice from the campanile of San Giorgio Maggiore, with La Pietà where Vivaldi played in the foreground. Because of his red hair, he was called the *prete rosso* (the Red Priest).

were obligatory, except for Venetian nobles. The island of Murano was another hotbed of gambling. During Carnival, when the high-rollers had lost all their money, they would gather in the workshops of the glassmakers to watch the objects being blown and to enjoy the heat from the kilns.

Until 1637 there were dozens of theatres that were privately owned, mainly by nobles. They put on the famous *commedie dell'arte*, improvised shows based on stock characters. Some people found them amusing while others thought them pitiable farces. Opera then became fashionable, proving so successful that more theatres were opened. Good music could also be enjoyed at the great religious services – for instance, the works of Claudio Monteverdi, a Venetian by adoption, whose magnificient State funeral took place in 1643 after he had spent the last thirty years of his life as choirmaster at St Mark's, composing sacred music and operas. And finally there were concert performances by the famous singing virtuosi from the four Venetian *ospedaletti* (hospices) – originally orphanages, which gradually developed into conservatoires.

The appointment of Antonio Vivaldi to a post at the Ospedale della Pietà provided him with a great opportunity for experimentation in the use of rare instruments. The Red Priest, as he was known on account of his hair colour, loved to conduct its female orchestra, for whom much of his

INDUSTRIAL ESPIONAGE

THE EXPERTISE OF VENETIAN GLASSBLOWERS was unique to the Serenissima. The first reference to a trade association dates from 1224 and concerns the punishment of thirty-odd people for violating the rules of secrecy which were imposed by the *Giustizia Vecchia* (Old Authority), which regulated the glassmakers. But the craftsmen themselves appear much earlier in Venice's history – a glassmaker is mentioned in a document from the year 982 alongside the names of the doge, the senior officials of the city and representatives of the various social classes. Windows, chandeliers, mirrors and vases were produced in increasing quantities by the master glassmakers to meet demand from the courts of Europe and the Orient. Work in the furnaces continued on a twelve-hour shift basis without interruption from January to August. Harsh though this might seem from the viewpoint of the twenty-first century, the labour regulations governing this exhausting and painstaking trade were more advanced than those in force elsewhere in contemporary Europe. To reduce the risk of damage to the city through fire, by the end of the thirteenth century production had gradually moved to the less densely populated island of Murano.

In the mid-seventeenth century the French ambassador to Venice offered some Murano masters much higher wages if they would go secretly to France. In a speech made by a da Mosto in those years to the *specchieri* (mirror-makers), he praised their art, implying that their 'pledge of obedience', or rule of secrecy imposed by the Republic, must be respected. The Venetian State Inquisitors sent out spies, and even poisoned one of the errant glassmakers, terrorizing the others into returning to Venice. But the French had already learnt some of their industrial secrets, and Murano glassmakers began to leave the city ever more frequently.

music was composed. Vivaldi led them with easy elegance; his students sang enchantingly and played all the orchestral instruments with supreme skill.

A less well-known Venetian composer, though very popular among his contemporaries, was Baldassare Galuppi, known as the Buranello because he was born on Burano island. Choirmaster in the hospice of the Mendicanti, he was later described in these terms: 'Galuppi showed no weakness towards the fair sex, he navigated his way around the sirens of the theatre, considerably more dangerous than those of the sea: but their fine figures, their sweet and gratifying features, their clever words, their angelic voices and graceful attitudes did not seduce him: and, as far as the public could

Above: An exquisite example of Murano glassware in my family home.

judge, without the need for Odysseus's wax, he cleverly resisted every enchantment.' He later became choirmaster at St Mark's Basilica, and his musical compositions included oratorios, concertos, sonatas for harpsichord and comic operas, including about thirty with libretti by the Venetian dramatist Goldoni.

The story goes that a certain nobleman who lived in a palace on the Grand Canal had a passion for music. He loved the trumpet and used to call his servants – of whom he had more than fifty – by playing the individual tune he had assigned to each one; unfortunately, he was a total amateur and confusion reigned. At first several servants would come running at once, but later they adopted the carefree catchphrase of Goldoni's comedies – 'Let him call!' – and no one turned up at all.

When he was a boy Goldoni joined a company of comedians heading for Chioggia and led a wandering life, after which he worked for many years at the Sant'Angelo theatre in Venice. His plays were extremely popular in all senses: they portrayed the types of the bustling *calli* and *campi* with total realism, using the lively and immediate language of Venetian dialect. The *Villeggiatura* (Holiday) trilogy describes the daily life of the mercantile and noble classes that were his inspiration, just as they were for his great friend Alessandro Longhi.

Longhi's paintings immerse the viewer in the daily life of the Venetian aristocracy. The stark formality of the previous two hundred years had now been definitively abandoned and in the eighteenth century the nobility favoured sensual, brightly coloured clothing. Silk was all the rage, often interwoven with gold or silver threads and decorated with precious stones and pearls. The men wore jackets that resembled women's clothing: tight at the waist and flared below. Their skin-tight breeches were cut short at the knee to show off white silk stockings and shoes adorned with gold or silver buckles or with pearls. The final touch was added by the *bauto*.

Longhi gives us detailed visual descriptions of sumptuous dining rooms, salons for music or card-playing, kitchens with teams of cooks and servants, and libraries where tutors gave lessons in literature or geography. The small daughters of noble families were like ladies in miniature, exquisitely dressed in rich, flower-patterned fabrics. The colours of the clothes took their names from the latest novelties, such as 'coffee grounds' and 'Spanish tobacco'; the colour known as 'angel's feather' was a bright red reminiscent of that used in some of Tiepolo's paintings.

There are magnificent images of noblewomen in their bedrooms, sipping hot chocolate in bed during a visit by the priest, or at their *toilette* with maids or valets, applying powder and perfume in abundance as a substitute for washing. Pale shades prevailed: powder added to the desirable whiteness of the face, against which diamonds and pearls sparkled. Their

Above: A mask shop today. Now staged primarily for the tourists, Carnival is an important source of revenue for the city.

hair would be adorned with a flower; later in the century voluminously piled coiffures came into fashion. After their faces and necks were powdered beauty spots were applied, their exact position depending on the message the lady wished to transmit. There was a precise code in these matters: placed near the eye, for example, the beauty spot meant 'I am irresistible'. Further accessories, such as a handbag or a fan, emphasized the vanity of these ladies.

THE BEGINNING OF THE END

In January 1782 Grand Duke Paul Petrovich, the future Tsar Paul I of Russia and his consort Maria Fyodorovna visited Venice under the names of the Counts of the North. They stayed in regally furnished rooms in the Leon Bianco inn, which had been set up in my family's old palace at Santi Apostoli, the Ca' da Mosto.

The visit was supposed to have been a great secret, but everyone was excitedly exclaiming: 'We're going to see the son of Catherine the Great!' The Venetians spared their Russian guests none of the city's splendours, transporting them in covered gondolas and giving them masks so that they could go around incognito. How many secrets have been concealed by those masks that covered the faces of Venetians and travellers for up to six months a year! At a magnificent event in St Mark's, a wave of the hand from the grand duchess triggered the release of a huge artificial dove that flew around the square, lighting a hundred flaming torches and finally coming to rest on a replica 40 metres (over 130 feet) high of the Arch of Titus in Rome.

Her husband was amazed by the discipline of the crowd, who were controlled by a mere five ushers from the Council of Ten rather than a regiment of soldiers. '*Voilà*,' he commented, 'the effect of the wise government of the Republic. This people is a family.' Despite their admiration for all things Venetian, however, certain aspects of the Russians' visit left much to be desired. They did not pay the entire bill for their accommodation, nor did they leave any tips at the Arsenale banquet – failing even to make a donation to the orphanage as was customary at the time.

The Leon Bianco hosted other illustrious visitors in the last decades of the Republic, among them the young Emperor Joseph II of Austria in 1769. The emperor tried to dissuade the Venetians from their grandiose plans in his honour, in particular the government's proposal to re-create the Gardens of the Hesperides in St Mark's Basin. It was to have occupied a platform 150 metres (492 feet) wide and to include a lake with live fish, flowers and crystal trees – but was intended to be no more than a prelude to a sumptuous banquet on the island of San Giorgio.

Although the project was not carried out, it had been planned down

to the last detail at considerable cost. This was enough to unleash a wave of bad feeling against the government, particularly among those young intellectuals who had begun to absorb the new ideas seeping in from France. The Republic had huge public debts, even after more than fifty years of relative peace, and even to consider such an undertaking seemed totally irresponsible.

But the State had no intention of allowing new-fangled ideas to penetrate its age-old ways of doing things. In 1783, for instance, the Senate rejected proposals for a trade and friendship treaty with the infant United States of America. Yet the banks were languishing and the Venetians, short of cash or having already lost it all, would sometimes even kneel down to take the jewelled buckles off their shoes to gamble them, before moving on to their rings, watches and even clothes. A certain Antonio Cestari was condemned to the oars for having staked his clothes and been left naked. 'Trade is sliding towards total decline, and there is not even a shadow of the old mercantile spirit among our citizens and subjects. The old enduring

Above: The front of the Ca' da Mosto today, where the Leon Bianco inn was situated in the eighteenth century.

maxims and laws that created and could still create a great state have been forgotten, there is no capital. And what still circulates in trade, rather than supporting or increasing industry, is used to maintain the comforts, excessive luxuries, vain shows, alleged amusements and vices.' This was how Andrea Tron, called *el paron* (the boss) because of his political influence, described the situation in the Senate on 29 May 1784, when an exciting distraction, a hot-air balloon, appeared in St Mark's Square.

The experiment carried out by the Montgolfier brothers in France in 1783 had aroused considerable interest among scientists and others. His Excellency Ser Francesco Pesaro, procurator of St Mark's, commissioned the Zanchi brothers to build an 'aerostatic globe with inflammable air'. It had a diameter of 20 Venetian feet and carried a 13-foot-long basket. The balloon was launched, though without passengers, on 15 April 1784 in St Mark's Basin. It went up successfully, staying in the air for about two and a half hours before coming down in the mud flats of the lagoon. A medal was minted to commemorate the event, and Francesco Guardi recorded the flight in a painting.

In February of the same year a nobleman named Farsetti had tried the same experiment in a garden on the island of San Giorgio. A large audience, including many other nobles, sat watching in eager anticipation, but the balloon, which was filled with 'inflammable air' for four hours, remained obstinately on the ground.

While the city appeared to have totally given itself up to vice and pleasure, the Barbary Coast pirates of the Bey of Tunisia returned to their old ways in response to damage suffered by Tunisian subjects in Malta, although through no fault of Venice. When diplomacy failed to smooth ruffled feathers, a Venetian naval squadron commanded by Angelo Emo was despatched. This was to be the Republic's last maritime action. Thanks to a new invention, floating gun batteries, that had no keels and could thus get very close to their objective, the Venetians were able to blockade Tunis. In 1786 the Bey was forced to sign a treaty safeguarding the seas from Barbary piracy. Unfortunately it turned out to be no more than a piece of paper and the pirates soon re-emerged. Meanwhile, warnings of far greater imminent upheaval and bloodshed were being sent by the Venetian ambassador in Paris.

AN ATTILA TO THE STATE OF VENICE

In January 1789 Lodovico Manin was elected doge in the most expensive election ever held. Manin was from a mainland family of recent nobility, and his election prompted the nobleman Piero Gradenigo to comment: *I ga fato dose un furlan, la Repubblica xe morta* ('A Friulano has been made doge, the

Previous pages left: In the late-eighteenth century the Venetian State was suffering financially and the city was in decline. When Napoleon threatened Venice in 1797 the days of the Republic were numbered.
Previous pages right: The home of Daniele Manin, who led the 1848 revolution against the Austrians in an attempt to regain independence for Venice. He took the Manin family name because he worked in their household.

Republic is dead'). In France the Revolution broke out that year, though it had scant effect on Venice. Only when the Revolutionary Wars began in the 1790s did the Serenissima have to take some sort of stance. In 1793 when Britain, the Netherlands and Spain were preparing for war against France, which was already fighting Austria, the Senate decided first on a policy of unarmed neutrality, then on one of armed neutrality.

Events followed hard upon one another, and the war between France and Austria threatened Italy. In 1795 the first misunderstandings arose between the two republics, French and Venetian, when the latter gave permission for the Comte de Lille to stay in Verona. He was the brother of Louis XVI, guillotined a couple of years earlier, and in the face of complaints from the revolutionary government the Senate felt obliged to ask him to leave.

The French advance was relentless. Piedmont fell and the Austrians were beaten in Lombardy; then Napoleon Bonaparte, commander of the French forces, attacked the fortress of Peschiera, which was under-equipped and offered little resistance. In order to pursue the Austrians he now crossed the border of the neutral Serenissima: 'The French army is passing through the Republic's territory,' he asserted, 'but will not forget the long friendship that unites the two republics.' Fine words, but … the French soon occupied Bergamo and Brescia, which were poorly defended. Then, thanks to collaborators among the local people and the timidity of the authorities, they also occupied the weakly protected hills of Verona.

In the campaign of the following year, Napoleon headed towards Austrian territory beyond the Alps. In the preliminaries to the treaty of Leoben, the terms of which he kept secret, the price of peace was Venetian territory to be ceded to Austria, though the Veneto state was allowed to survive in limited form: the city of Venice and the lagoon.

At the end of 1796 the French occupied the region as far as the River Adige; Vicenza, Cadore and Friuli were held by the Austrians. The following Easter a terrible insurrection against the French broke out, known as the *Pasqua Veronese* (Veronese Easter). The citizens of Verona fought bravely, but at the same time gave Napoleon an excuse to suppress the entire Venetian Republic. Things were now falling rapidly to pieces. Napoleon threatened Venice itself, declaring to the Venetian delegates in Graz: 'I will have no more Inquisition, no more Senate. I will be an Attila to the State of Venice.'

Having taken Verona, the French seized Vicenza and Padua and approached Mestre to get to Venice; an earlier advance from the sea had failed. On the evening of 30 April Doge Manin and his advisers nervously debated the gravity of the situation, and on 1 May Napoleon published his manifesto of war against the Republic. On 12 May, two days before the

Above: A print from my home showing Napoleon taking down the four bronze horses from St Mark's Basilica, which he then transported to Paris. Opposite: Napoleon destroyed the whole west end of St Mark's Square and replaced it with a palace (now the Correr Museum). Its central feature was this ballroom, which brought a slice of French neo-classical style to Venice.

expiry of the French ultimatum, the Great Council met, though with insufficient voters to form a quorum. Outside, a group of Slav sailors who were about to embark on their ship fired their muskets into the air as a salute. The noise frightened the council, which, to cries of 'Enough, enough, start, start!', approved the transfer of power to the 'system of the proposed provisional representative government'. One of the many named Vettor da Mosto, eighty years old and among the oldest senators, witnessed this moment when the Republic breathed its last; Count of Pola and one of the three leaders of the Quarantia Criminale, he was one of the few to stay with the doge after this last session of the Great Council. On 16 May French troops entered Venice, the 'provisional democratic municipality' was established and the Venetian democracy was dissolved by decree. The French–Austrian treaty of Campoformio reinforced the Leoben agreement: Venice and all its territories became Austrian.

Napoleon and his family may have supplied Canova, a great Venetian sculptor, with many commissions (see above), but in no way did this make up for the looting that now took place in the city. The French took the four bronze horses from St Mark's Basilica back to Paris, along with other valuable objects, under the pretext of saving them 'from the horrors of war'. The horses were later returned to Venice thanks to Austrian intervention, but many other masterpieces have yet to be returned.

CANOVA, THE SUPREME NEO-CLASSICIST

ANTONIO CANOVA, born in Possagno in 1757, began his apprenticeship with his grandfather, a local stone-cutter and sculptor of moderate renown. From the age of about seven Antonio is said to have shown a natural inclination for sculpture, moulding small objects out of clay. At a dinner attended by Venetian nobles in a villa in Asolo he made a lion from butter, which amazed all the guests. The head of the household arranged for him to join a nearby workshop, after which he went to Venice to continue his training.

In 1779 his marble group *Daedalus and Icarus* won him a prize, which enabled him to study in Rome. Here he produced some of his most beautiful works: *Love and Psyche*, *Adonis and Venus*, and *Hebe*. In his methods he copied the Ancient Greeks, moving from an initial drawing to clay, then to plaster and finally to marble. This approach also drew him closer to classical mythology: 'I work all day like a brute,' he said, 'but it is also true that almost every day I listen to readings from the tomes of Homer.'

When the French occupied Rome in 1798 he returned to Possagno and devoted himself to painting. But the arrival of Napoleon on the European political stage, and his coronation as emperor in 1804, marked the beginning of a fertile period in Canova's career – even though he disapproved of the French looting of Italian works of art.

In 1804, back in Rome, he completed the celebrated sculpture of *Paolina Borghese as Venus Victrix*; the sitter was Napoleon's sister, the wife of the Roman prince Camillo Borghese. Two years later Canova carved the famous statue of Napoleon now in Apsley House, London, the former home of Napoleon's arch-antagonist the Duke of Wellington; the emperor refused to let it be shown in public because of its explicit nudity.

Canova resisted the invitations to become artist to the French imperial court but he did go to Paris in 1815 when terms were being negotiated after the Battle of Waterloo. It was thanks to his skilful diplomacy that numerous valuable works of art purloined by Napoleon were returned to Italy.

Above: A lion of St Mark on Canova's monument in the church of Santa Maria Gloriosa dei Frari. Opposite: The ornate exterior of the Scuola Grande di San Marco that Napoleon transformed into Venice's *ospedale* – still the city's main hospital.

When Austrian troops entered Venice in triumph the bells in St Mark's Campanile remained silent: this was not a time for rejoicing but a deeply traumatic event. It affected the nobility in particular. Some families produced few or no offspring because they no longer wanted their name to be perpetuated. Others bowed to the inevitable: in 1798 my forebear Natale da Mosto was one of the nobles who vowed allegiance to the Austrian emperor. In 1802 Lodovico Manin, the last doge, died, and thus the last bulwark of the Republic passed away.

Poor Venice was tossed around like a plaything between the powers.

In 1806 French troops once again entered the city: Napoleon had achieved
victories that enabled him to sign a new treaty under which Venice and
the Veneto passed from Austria to his newly created Kingdom of Italy.
But things fell apart once again: Austria and its allies entered Milan in
1814 and declared the Kingdom of Italy over, so Venice returned to
Austrian dominion. The seal was finally set after the Battle of Waterloo
in 1815, when the Congress of Vienna gave all the Lombardy-Veneto
Kingdom, with its capital in Milan, to Austria. For the inhabitants of this
region, it marked the beginning of a new period of suppression.

THE CAMPANILE
OF ST MARK'S
AND ITS BELLS

THE FIVE PRINCIPAL BELLS of St Mark's –
the *Marangona*, the *Nona*, the
Mezzaterza, the *Trottiera* and the
Renghiera – used to regulate both
religious life and the affairs of city
and State. They announced meetings
of the Great Council, the Senate and
various tribunals; the changing of
the guard in St Mark's Square; the
election and death of doges, popes,
procurators and great chancellors;
the death of the doge's wife and sons,
of ambassadors, cardinals and the
patriarch; the return of galleys from
voyages; death sentences; the start
and end of the working day; and so
on. A 1582 guide to Venice gives this
lively description of the Campanile:

*It doesn't seem a thing of stone, but
one with feeling and spirit, at times
it cries, at times it laughs, sometimes
it speaks loudly and sometimes you
can't hear it. It weeps and sighs when
the crime bell rings, and laughs with
the double chime of happiness; it*
speaks loudly with the bora *[northeast
wind] and softly with the* scirocco
*[southwest wind] … It calls and
wakes all sorts of people: on feast
days it calls the doge to mass …
at vespers the priests, at dawn the
doctors … the lawyers and notaries to
the palace, at sunrise the craftsmen,
at sunset the artisans and on the day
of Corpus Domini, all the clergy.*

Apart from their regular chime
marking the hours, the bells of the
Campanile now ring out only on
religious occasions and on the death
and election of popes. Other bells,
one in the church of San Giacomo
di Rialto, used to be rung to signal
the end of the day's work for certain
categories of workers, and another,
further away in the church of San
Francesco della Vigna, announced the
end of Carnival and the beginning
of Lent.

Above left: One of the Campanile
bells, known as *la Marangona*, which
rings out every day.
Above: St Mark's Square with its
imposing Campanile.

For pleasure seekers, Venice in its decadence afforded, if anything, even more delights than ever. In 1816, following a scandal regarding an incestuous affair with his half-sister, the poet Byron arrived in the city, having crossed Europe in an enormous carriage built in imitation of Napoleon's. In 'Childe Harold's Pilgrimage' he vividly describes Venice in its dying glory, kept alive through its art:

> The spouseless Adriatic mourns her lord;
> And annual marriage now no more renew'd,
> The Bucentaur lies rotting unrestor'd,
> Neglected garment of her widowhood!
> St Mark yet sees his lion where he stood
> Stand, but in mockery of his wither'd power,
> Over the proud Place where an Emperor sued,
> And monarchs gaz'd and envied in the hour
> When Venice was a queen with an unequall'd dower.
> The Suabian sued, and now the Austrian reigns –
> An Emperor tramples where an Emperor knelt;
> Kingdoms are shrunk to provinces, and chains
> Clank over sceptred cities, nations melt
> From power's high pinnacle, when they have felt
> The sunshine for a while, and downward go
> Like lauwine loosen'd from the mountain's belt:
> Oh, for one hour of blind old Dandolo,
> Th' octogenarian chief, Byzantium's conquering foe!

In 1818 Byron moved to the Palazzo Mocenigo with fourteen servants, two monkeys, five cats, eight dogs, a crow, a sparrow-hawk, two parrots and a fox, fulfilling his dream of living in a house on the Grand Canal. For debauched eccentrics like him, the city was far from desolate: the Carnival was still fun and there were plenty of beautiful, adoring and available women. He was in constant demand in the *conversazione* salons, where acclaimed artists were welcomed by the most prominent ladies of the city. At the San Beneto theatre Byron encountered one Elena da Mosta – a noblewoman, or perhaps simply a courtesan who had assumed a noble name, a common practice at the time. For Lord Byron she was to prove a dangerous love.

While seeing Countess Isabella Teotochi Albrizzi at the theatre, where works by Haydn and Handel were being played, Lord Byron regretfully announced that he had to leave because of an urgent engagement. He had actually fallen prey to the agonies and torments of a new *amour*: da Mosta. He described her to his friend Samuel Rogers: a marvellous, wild head of

Above: The twin Palazzi Mocenigo where Byron lived with his menagerie on the Grand Canal.

THE LANGUAGE OF VENICE

—————

VENICE IS UNIQUE in its language, which, despite modern cultural influences from all over the world, remains stubbornly original, vital, expressive and fully up-to-date, being spoken and used regularly by all classes of society. Venetians are always ready to point out that their language should not be considered a mere local dialect, since in Republican times it was used in official documents, including magisterial proclamations by doges. There is also a considerable body of literature written in Venetian.

Visitors may sometimes get the idea that the language serves to protect the Venetian identity and they may even suspect that Venetians use it in the defensive way that street gangs use their own private jargons. This would be a mistake – Venetian remains quite simply the natural form of communication for most of the city's inhabitants. The language naturally has developed over the centuries and, in the practical way of all things Venetian, it has learned to adapt to changing circumstances.

In Venice's distant past the mainland peoples who first settled the lagoon, long before the tribal invasions from the North and East made it a necessity, would have spoken a Greek or near-Greek dialect, possibly Paphlagonian, reflecting their origins. Gradually, as the influence of Rome spread throughout the Italian peninsula, languages such as Celtic and Etruscan died out in favour of Latin. The Venetians accepted the new language, mixing and modifying it with accents and softenings from their Greek background. They also Latinized a number of terms that were still unknown elsewhere in Italy. Many of these came from Greek: *piron*, fork; *carega*, chair, from *carex* or *carice*, a material used to weave chairs; a word for lion, *moleca*, meaning literally 'majesty', was derived from *malacoseon*; *androne*, entrance hall, comes from *andrononos*, house of man. The later, Eastern, influences are evident in the proliferation of the letters X and Z. This, indeed, is turned to advantage: *xe*, meaning 'is', though pronounced *se*, cannot be confused in the written language with *se* meaning 'if'. Among other words that came from the East was the name of the Venetian mint, the Zecca, derived from the Arabic word *sikka*, the die from which a coin was cast, while *Arsenale* (arsenal) derives from the Arabic 'dar sinaa', a workshop, where ships were built.

Cross-currents of linguistic influence are evident throughout the Mediterranean and regions further east where Venice was influential. In the days when the Venetians and Genoese traded in the Black Sea, Italian was the language of business in some ports in southern Russia. In Istria and along the Dalmatian coast of the

hair, sea–blue eyes and an insatiable appetite for love. He also remarked that she had given him the only dose of gonorrhoea he had not had to pay for – adding philosophically that when one is young it is better to die 'in battle'.

My search in the family archives for information on this impassioned courtesan was frustrating. I could find no documents relating to wills or property, and unfortunately the affair had occured twenty years after the demise of the Republic, by which time its marvellous archives and filing system had fallen into disuse. Help came at last from an archive of the Austrian Heraldic Commission in which an Elena Elisabetta da Mosto is named (da Mosta could be a natural variation of the same name). She married Girolamo Savorgnan in the church of San Luca on 20 October 1824,

—————

Pages 192–3: The twin Palazzi Mocenigo where Byron lived with his menagerie on the Grand Canal.

Adriatic the indigenous populations had to cope with Croat on land and Venetian at sea. In 1553 Giovambattista Giustiniani inspected the eastern Adriatic military bases on behalf of the Republic and witnessed Slav-Romanic bilingualism in Dalmatia. He observed that the *lingua franca* was spoken at Pirano, Zara, Sebenico and Lesina, whereas in Spalato (modern Split) 'everyone speaks the *lingua franca* but the womenfolk don't sparkle unless in their mother tongue'. Reports from Ragusa (now Dubrovnik) suggested that the *lingua franca* was the same as that used by Christians in Eastern Mediterranean ports to communicate with Arabs and Turks.

Francesco Sansovino, son of the famous architect, reinforced this view in 1607:

Regarding language, each youth [male] normally knew the Italian language [and] these [inhabitants of Ragusa] call it 'Franca': but amongst themselves they use only their own mother tongue … They invite likewise every year an excellent preacher, who preaches only to the men, and this because they preach in Italian, which the women don't understand.

Rich in idioms, and in its own lively and original terms derived from an abundance of sources, the Venetian language has always favoured ease of use and simplification. It tries to avoid the double consonants, such as *ss* or *tt*, which appear frequently in conventional Italian – if something is broken elsewhere in Italy it is *rotto*, but in Venice it is *roto*; and Venetians disregard the letter L so that, for example, *bello* becomes *beo*, rendering perfectly ordinary words sometimes quite incomprehensible to foreigners.

Abbreviations abound: one of the first that tourists encounter is *Ca'*, short for *Casa*, meaning literally 'house' but more sensibly nowadays translated as 'palace', as in Ca' d'Oro, Ca' da Mosto and so on. Suffixes such as 'o', 'i' and 'a' tend to be dropped – which I interpret as Venetian laziness. Thus Venice's history abounds with patrician names such as Venier, Falier and Badoer, which to the uninitiated may sound very un-Italian, and although the city produced a fifteenth-century Queen of Cyprus known as Caterina Cornaro, other members of her family are known more prosaically as Corner. Some of the contractions of complex or long-winded names are baffling to outsiders, although we Venetians take them for granted. So perhaps they are best described in the words of a legendary foreign resident in the city, Jan Morris, who wrote in Venice:

You may look, consulting your guide book, for the church of Santi Giovanni e Paolo; but the street sign will call it San Zanipolo … What the Venetians call San Stae is really Sant' Eustacchio. San Stin is Santo Stefano. Sant' Aponal is Sant' Apollinare.

the year Byron went to Greece and died. Perhaps it really was an important love affair as he did have a weakness for women with Corfiot blood. Elena's mother was Countess Leonilda Bulgari, whose family came from Corfu.

Byron was a famous swimmer. His best-known exploit was crossing the Hellespont, and in Venice he is said to have swum along the Grand Canal at night in pursuit of his many scandalous affairs. He often went to the Lido, where he kept his horses, and it was from there that he apparently suggested a race for those of his friends able to swim back to Venice and then the full length of the Grand Canal – a total of more than 7 kilometres (over 4 miles). There are varying versions of the story; unsurprisingly, Byron's own boasted that he had beaten all the other competitors, including a veteran

Above and opposite:
After the fall of the
Republic, Venice's decline
continued. But Byron and
other writers and artists,
both of his era and years
later, were inspired by
the romance of the
city's forgotten streets
and palaces, and its
atmosphere of crumbling
decadence.

of the Napoleonic campaigns who claimed to have swum across both the
Beresina and the Danube during the retreat from Russia.

But while Byron and his ilk played, gambled and whored, Venice
under Austrian rule was in a parlous state. Its population had fallen,
unemployment was on the rise, hunger and poverty were rife. The city
was full of abandoned and decaying houses and palaces as the fortunes of
the noble families just dwindled away. The Arsenale was falling to pieces
and boats were being broken up. Grass grew between the paving stones,
and the historic artistic heritage had been ransacked. However, such decay
merely added to its powerful romantic attraction to foreigners, enchanting
artists and writers with its decadent atmosphere. Byron described it to his
fellow poet Thomas Moore as the 'greenest island of my imagination'.

5

ETHER

LIFE UNDER UNCERTAINTY

When I was a schoolboy, in order to explain the shape and geography of Italy, my teachers drew it as a boot; later, as a logo for the soccer World Cup, it remained a boot but with a ball, Sicily, and a Mexican sombrero on its head. Venice has always had the shape of a headless fish. Alas, my childhood innocence was destroyed when I started seeing it as a fish on a hook. I am referring to the bridge built under Austrian rule that hooks the city to the mainland, to the continent, to the land of foreigners. There are moments when I feel Venice writhing on that hook, pulled at high speed by the baited line that draws it ever closer.

Then the industrial mainland, like an implacable fisherman, eases the line, forced to do so by the fierce strength of this creature, its tail emerging from the water like a great blade refracting the sunlight into a rainbow of gleaming colours. But the struggle goes on, and at times I am afraid the city will succumb to creeping industrialization.

As I gaze out towards the mainland, a gondolier speaks to me in dialect and my mind drifts back three centuries to an episode at the end of the eighteenth century, when the lagoon was frozen over and Venice could be reached by coach and horses – when meteorology rather than engineering joined it for a while to the mainland. Just one year before the French Revolution and a few before the fall of the Republic, pleasure-seeking was still the city's *raison d'être*. It was Carnival time, and a ball held in honour of the King of Denmark and Norway had to be curtailed to enable the guests to return home before the canals froze. A visitor enthused that they 'sparkled in the rays of the sun

Opposite: The 'hook' that links Venice to the mainland, ironically named *Ponte della Libertà* (Bridge of Freedom).

and moon like mirrors or diamonds', and a painting from Guardi's studio recorded the scenes for posterity. All tariffs were temporarily removed so that food and other necessities could arrive in sufficient quantity. Venice experienced the unusual sight of herds of cows, flocks of sheep and droves of pigs crossing the ice from the mainland; barrels of wine and drinking water were rolled over the great glistening white surface, while wicker hampers, sacks of flour and bundles of firewood were carried on people's backs or on horse-drawn sledges.

In the past twelve centuries the whole lagoon and most of the canals have frozen over nineteen times, most recently in 1929. It was Doge Marco Foscarini in the 1760s who first conceived the bold idea of joining Venice permanently to the mainland. A distinguished scholar, he had a deep understanding of his native city and, all too aware of its increasing languor and decrepitude, he envisaged the project as a way of countering the decline in trade. But the Senate was horrified by the idea; its members had not yet lost hope that Venice might regain its power over the seas. Even in the early nineteenth century, when the city's economic and commercial situation had deteriorated even further because the Austrian rulers favoured the port of Trieste, the idea of a bridge still aroused opposition among reactionaries who believed that Venice could somehow survive in splendid isolation. One of these was Giambattista Gavin Manocchi:

Venice was born as an island, it grew as an island, it became rich and magnificent as an island, and it is suited to no other condition than as an island, with internal canals for boats to use, because by origin, chance and constitution it is unlike any other city in the world. Venice had no need of bridges in the past because it flourished

Above: Francesco Battaglioli's painting of 1788 shows how life continued for the Venetians despite the frozen lagoon. This event inspired the idea for a permanent link to the mainland, to which many citizens were opposed. Opposite: Until 1837 bridges in Venice were only conceived to criss-cross the inner canals and weave together its constituent islands and islets.

marvellously without them, apart from those within it that connect up the group of islets of which it is composed; and it has no need of one at the present time.

Among the various proposals put forward was that of a wood merchant, who proposed building a wooden bridge at his own expense, with shops, garages and stables. In exchange, he asked the government for a certain number of prisoners to construct it and to be allowed to demand a toll for himself and his heirs for fifty years. Another plan, for a railway bridge crossing the lagoon to a station on the island of San Giorgio Maggiore, with trains steaming right into St Mark's Basin in the heart of the city, was considered very audacious. Instead in 1837 the definitive plan was approved, and Venice's link with the mainland and the railway line to Milan was set in motion (see page 202). Less than one hundred years later a road bridge was added alongside it.

STEAMPOWER AND GASLIGHT: VENICE ENTERS THE INDUSTRIAL AGE

THE LONG-AWAITED BRIDGE over the lagoon was opened on 13 January 1846 in the presence of Archduke Ferdinand of Austria and Count Giovanni Correr, *podestà* of Venice. The *Gazzetta* newspapaper reported:

The authorities gathered at 9.45 inside the station. But the hour of departure was already sounding in the roar of billowing steam; the engine, triumphantly decorated, was hooked on to the wagons: and she, the first to escort Venice into its

embrace with the mainland, is named after the Bucintoro, *as in other days another* Bucintoro *used to escort her to her mystical marriage with the sea.*

The exultant tone testifies to the enthusiasm for the new enterprise, which involved the entire population. A few years after the opening of the railway it was said that Venice 'seems to have been miraculously resurrected, her population has expanded, old factories have been repaired and new ones built; and her streets have become so busy that she appears to have returned to the happier days of her envied power'.

But for the romantics among Venice's visitors, the sense of nineteenth-

century energy and progress that now characterized the city shattered their dreams. One such was the writer and art critic John Ruskin, whose most famous work, *The Stones of Venice* (1851–3), outraged some people as he appeared to regard decoration in architecture as more important than structure. Venetian Gothic, he thought, was the pinnacle of architectural achievement. A letter which Ruskin sent home to his father describes the newly modernized city in tones of despair and incredulity:

It began to look a little better as we got up to the Rialto, but, it being just solemn twilight, as we turned under the arch, behold, all up to the Foscari palace – gas lamps! On each side, grand new iron posts of the last Birmingham fashion, and sure enough, they have them all up the narrow canals, and there is a grand one, with more flourishes than usual, just under the Bridge of Sighs. Imagine the new style of serenades … by gas light.

1848: THE SERENISSIMA IN REVOLT

In the 1840s a combination of repressive governments and nationalistic awakening led to a series of revolutions across Europe. In Venice the economic and social problems that had affected the city in recent years, aggravated by the broader European crisis, had been creating widespread discontent and serious hardship. Taxes and duties imposed by the Austrian administration, shortages of essential items, rising prices and the collapse of many businesses all added to the general malaise. In 1847 the ninth conference of Italian scientists was held in the city. A stimulus for revolutionary intellectuals, it was also an occasion to protest against Austrian domination and to celebrate the former independence of the Venetian Republic. The lagoon bridge, the new physical link with the mainland, was to be the scene of Venice's final act of resistance to the imperial army in the uprisings of 1848–9.

Events began with the arrest of Daniele Manin, an eloquent lawyer who, striving to uphold the rights of the people and to assert Venetian independence, had stood up to the occupiers, and Nicolò Tommaseo, a celebrated patriotic writer and scholar. During a popular uprising in which the prisons were stormed the two leaders were freed and taken triumphantly around the city. Italian officers and soldiers then defected from the Austrian army, whose forces had to retreat behind the walls of Verona. The Venetian historian Cicogna recorded an anonymous parody of the Lord's Prayer which was composed at this time: 'Father Metternich [the Austrian chancellor] who art in Vienna, cursed be thy name, thy kingdom perish, thy will not be done, on earth as it is in heaven, thou hast stolen our daily bread, forgive us our trespasses as we forgive thine, lead us not into temptation of rebellion, but deliver us from all evil with thy death, Amen.'

On 23 March, the liberation of the city and its hinterland, and the inauguration of a provisional government of the Venetian republic, were formally proclaimed in St Mark's Square: 'Citizens! In accordance with protocol, the current repository of power, fulfilling the mandate assumed with the aim of benefiting the interests of the homeland, proposes for public approval a provisional government composed of the following citizens … ' The first two names were those of Tommaseo and Manin. Many Venetians offered practical support: my great-great-grandfather Andrea da Mosto gave all the family's silverware, as well as money.

The powerful Austrian army soon organized a counter-offensive against the weaker forces of the defiant Italian cities, Venice in particular. Over the following months it gradually reoccupied the whole of the Veneto mainland, and in May 1849 attacked Fort Marghera on the outskirts of Mestre. In order to slow down the Austrian advance, the Venetians decided to blow up five arches of the railway bridge. A gun battery was set up on the end of the mutilated structure, which became the symbol of Venice's resistance. At the end of July, with the desperate citizens enduring starvation and cholera, the Austrians began a heavy bombardment. On 19 August 1849 terms of surrender were agreed, which stipulated the exile of the provisional government. Five days later Venice was forced to capitulate, although having won the admiration of the whole world.

Above: 'Huge, inhuman and monstrous, leering in bestial degradation, too foul to be either pictured or described'. This was how John Ruskin described this stone head on the base of the campanile of Santa Maria Formosa. Opposite: Lovers of the city's traditional architecture, including Ruskin, despaired of the introduction of modern inventions, such as gas lamps.

Ca' Rezzonico
Museo del Settecento Veneziano
Pinacoteca Egidio Martini
Collezione Mestrovich

A MAGNET FOR VICTORIAN WRITERS

DURING THE UPRISINGS OF 1848–9 Venice's perennial attraction for intellectuals and artists had, of course, temporarily ceased. John Ruskin only returned when the hotels were operating once more under Austrian regulations, this time with his new wife, Effie. While she moved in the highest circles of society and gallant officers duelled for the favour of dancing with her, Ruskin once again immersed himself in his studies and his writing. His letters give the impression that this was one of the happiest times of his life:

I rise at half past six; am dressed by seven – take a little bit of bread, and read till nine then we have breakfast punctually: very orderly served – a little marmalade with a silver leafage spoon on a coloured tile at one corner of the table – butter very fresh – in ice – grapes and figs – which I never touch; on one side – peaches on the other – also for ornament chiefly – (I never take them) – a little hot dish, which the cook is bound to furnish every morning – a roast beccafaco [a small bird – a particular delicacy] – or other little tiny kickshaw – before Effie white bread and coffee. Then I read Pope or play by myself till 10 – when we have prayer: and Effie reads to me and I draw till eleven: then I write till one when we have

lunch: then I go out, and sketch or take notes till three – then row for an hour and a half – come in and dress for dinner at 5, play by myself till seven – sometimes out on the water again in an idle way: tea at seven – write or draw till nine – and get ready for bed.

The idyll was one-sided. As a husband, Ruskin was a dismal failure. Later, the marriage was annulled.

Very different from the Ruskins' relationship were those of two other literary couples who found inspiration in Venice.

The Venetian atmosphere attracted George Eliot (the pseudonym of Mary Ann Evans). A farmer's daughter who was brought up as an evangelical Christian, she later distanced herself from religion and in middle age became the most celebrated English novelist of the day, author of

Middlemarch, *Silas Marner* and *The Mill on the Floss*. The American writer Henry James was to write of Eliot: 'She was magnificently, awe-inspiringly ugly.' In 1880 she married John Cross, twenty years her junior, who was also her administrator. In Venice they stayed at the Hotel Europa from which, whether by accident or design, Cross fell into the Grand Canal and had to be rescued by a gondolier. He may have been fleeing his new wife's advances: although no beauty, she was notoriously highly sexed!

Many of Robert Browning's most intense poems are on Italian themes. He first visited the country in 1838 and returned in 1846 to settle in Florence for fifteen years with his wife and fellow-poet Elizabeth Barrett Browning, who wrote her magnum opus *Aurora Leigh* in Italy. One of his finest poems on a Venetian subject is 'A Toccata of Galuppi's', which refers to the composer from Burano. After his wife's death in 1861 Browning returned to England, but he continued to visit Venice on a regular basis. The Ca' Rezzonico was to be his last residence in the city: he died there on 12 December 1889.

Opposite: The baroque Ca' Rezzonico, the last Venetian home of the poet Robert Browning.
Above: A sketch (c.1850) by John Ruskin of the Doge's Palace with the Basilica behind.

THE WARS OF INDEPENDENCE

After the sixteen months of insurrection in 1848–9, coinciding with the first Italian war of independence from French, Austrian and Bourbon-Spanish rule, an exhausted Venice found itself once again under the Austrian yoke. When Daniele Manin died in exile in Paris in 1857 one of the leading figures of the 1848 revolution wrote: 'We do not ask that Austria become more human – we just want it to go.' Over the next decade or so the various European powers and the small foreign-dominated Italian states indulged in mutual back-scratching to achieve their individual objectives – for the former, to gain ascendancy over their rivals on the European political stage, and for the latter, to gain independence and the unification of Italy.

The independence movement, known as the *Risorgimento* (resurrection), was centred on the Kingdom of Piedmont-Sardinia with its capital in Turin. The hopes raised in 1859 by the second war of independence and the victories of the Piedmontese and their ally Napoleon III of France over the Austrians were dashed by the terms agreed by the French to end the

Below: A nineteenth-century lithograph of skirmishes during the 1848 Venetian revolution against the Austrians.

conflict, which took Lombardy into Piedmont-Sardinia but left the Veneto to Austria. However, the following year, with the tacit assistance of the British navy, the revolutionary leader Giuseppe Garibaldi landed in Sicily with his thousand 'Red Shirts'. He encouraged the local people to rise up against the Bourbon Kingdom of the Two Sicilies, and that same year delivered the whole of southern Italy, including Naples, to the Kingdom of Piedmont-Sardinia which, in 1861, became the Kingdom of Italy.

Venetian challenges to foreign occupation became more marked in these years – but so did the repression. The third war of independence, fought against Austria in 1866 in an attempt to annex the Veneto, was preceded by a dreadful financial crisis. The Italians then suffered two humiliating defeats, on land at Custozza and at sea at Lissa, but their allies, the more powerful Prussians, were victorious at Sadowa. However, the Austrians obstinately refused to cede Venice and the Veneto to Italy in the subsequent peace treaty. They went instead to France – which then handed these territories over, like a bill of exchange, to King Victor Emmanuel II of Italy. And so, after sixty-seven years of foreign rule and a referendum of dubious validity, Venice regained its freedom, if not its independence, when Italian troops entered the city in October. This move was not, however, universally popular, and some considered it an act of force and deception to annex a state, the Republic of Venice, which for a thousand years had given glory to Italy and Europe and to the entire Mediterranean.

A CITY OF THE NEW ITALY

At the time of the 1848 uprising my great-great-grandfather Andrea da Mosto, a lonely widower, had given the equivalent of tens of millions of euros in support of his fellow-countrymen who opposed the Austrians. He was not alone: the cost of the wars of independence brought the whole city to its knees. The Teatro La Fenice remained closed from 1848 to 1866 because the families who had formerly hired the boxes and made the place economically viable were now living in greatly reduced circumstances. Meanwhile, Andrea's son Antonio was a favoured chamberlain to Emperor Franz Joseph and was based in Parenzo, Istria. This extract from a letter from father to son is a vivid account of those times. It was written in 1877.

Dearest Son,
It was with much pleasure that I received your dear letter yesterday, having awaited it eagerly, and learn with satisfaction how you were kindly welcomed by the emperor and his ministers. These are comforts that are only obtained from Austria, which well knows how to value the merits and useful services of its employees, of which here no account is made …

Overleaf: Contemporary Venice, looking towards the church of Santi Giovanni e Paolo, flanked by the hospital's unmistakeable Renaissance façade. The cemetery island of San Michele, with its cypresses, and the island of Murano lie beyond, while the lagoon stretches into the distance.

Although nothing positive can be said about the situation in the East, I always maintain that developments will be peaceful, despite everyone being contrary to this opinion of mine and thinking that war is imminent. I may be wrong, but I cannot persuade myself that Russia can have decided to occupy the Turkish states with force, nor that the Powers, especially England, could leave its survival to chance, having always supported it not out of sympathy but to ensure European equilibrium. It is also not to be believed that the Powers could show themselves indifferent to Russia's moves …

I hear that General Jgnasief will go to Vienna, Berlin and Paris in order to come to terms in some way with those Powers that have not yet responded to the Gonciakof Circular, and who, by their silence, show that they are not persuaded to support Russian policy. I think that a way will be found to avoid the conflict, and that the condition of the Christians subject to Turkey will be guaranteed. You will tell me how strange it is that, without any grounding in politics, I allow myself to predict that which not even statesmen are able to foretell and you will be right, but whether it be due to my desire to see peace maintained, or to my own premonition, I continue to think that the current difficulties will end peacefully, at least for the moment.

After all this talk, I intend not to say another word on this subject, and we will see how it ends, but if, amid the general belief that war is inevitable, my forecasts should come true, I would be very satisfied and content. [War did, in fact, break out.]

To bring you up to date on the closing of the Teatro della Fenice … the contractor disappeared at the end of Carnival … the money collected by the company for the Carnival spectacles had already been spent … no one could predict the collapse and … the theatre's directorship was very imprudent in trusting the company without covering itself, but … on the other hand the owners of the boxes cannot be blamed, after all they had paid, for refusing to make up for the expenses necessary to enable the theatre to stay open during Lent …

In its first twenty 'Italian' years Venice's municipal administration was unable to revive the city's flagging financial fortunes. It remained exhausted after decades of crisis, despite attempts to relaunch the port, to stimulate commerce and to industrialize. Meanwhile, the erosion of the city's cultural heritage, which had begun under Napoleon, continued unabated as works of art, other treasures, books and documents were sold off to foreigners, for Venice was still on their cultural itineraries and still played the role of inspirational muse to writers, artists and musicians.

Towards the end of the nineteenth century left-wing liberals and radicals created initiatives to relaunch Venice with town-planning schemes and with commercial, educational and social projects, such as 'healthy, cheap municipal housing' for the poorer members of society. Studies were carried out into the feasibility of building an industrial estate outside the city. All the various modernizing schemes that gave Venice its present appearance were first proposed in this period: the development of hotels and of beach

WAGNER IN VENICE

THE FIRST IMPRESSION that the impoverished, mid-nineteenth-century city made on the German composer Richard Wagner was one of desolate abandonment, but it proved to be also a treasure trove of dreams and desires, of beauty and wonder. His autobiography, diary and letters provide a series of images and observations that allow us to see the city through his eyes over twenty-five years of regular visits. They immerse us in his moods, his work, the company of his children and the depth of his relationship with his second wife Cosima.

Some words from his *Venetian Diary* of 1858, the year when he completed his opera *Tristan und Isolde*, reflect his feelings. Where John Ruskin a decade or so earlier had been appalled at what he regarded as hideous anachronisms, such as gas lighting, Wagner found no such horrors.

I arrived in Venice on the afternoon of 29 August. During the trip down the Grand Canal to the Piazzetta, melancholy impressions, serious, pensive mood: grandeur, beauty and decay at the same time before my eyes. It was comforting to me to reflect that here there is no sign of modern prosperity; so no commercial vulgarity. St Mark's Square is like a fairy-tale. A totally remote world, of other times: everything harmonizes excellently with my desire for solitude. Nothing here seems to be in direct contact with real life; everything acts objectively like a work of art. I want to stay here, and will stay here.

In 1882, after the premiere of *Parsifal* at Bayreuth, Wagner returned to Venice and occupied an apartment in the sixteenth-century Ca' Vendramin Calergi, where he was eventually to die. A plaque on the wall of what is today the municipal casino commemorates him in the words of the poet Gabriele D'Annunzio: 'In this palace the spirits hear the last breath of Richard Wagner perpetuate itself, like the tide lapping the marbles.'

Above: The last home of Richard Wagner, who visited Venice regularly for twenty-five years.

ST MARK'S CAMPANILE, HEAD OF THE VENETIAN HOUSEHOLD

THE CAMPANILE, popularly known as *il paron di casa* (the head of the household), has had a long, eventful history. It was begun around 900 and work continued through subsequent centuries under various architects, including Nicolò Barattieri, the man who built the first wooden bridge at the Rialto. In 1489 lightning struck the tower. It was rebuilt by Bartolomeo Bon, who added an attic and spire.

Tournaments, bull chases and other festivities were held in the Piazza. One entertainment was known as the Flight of the Dove. A rope was stretched from an anchored boat to the top of the Campanile and another descended from it, over the Piazzetta, to the loggia of the Doge's Palace. By means of a system of pulleys a man dressed as an angel was hauled up from the boat to the Campanile, then 'flew' down via the second rope, scattering flowers. On reaching the loggia, he presented the doge with flowers and a dedication in verse, receiving in exchange a bag of money. He then 'flew' back up to the top of the Campanile and down to the boat. Today, a scaled-down 'flight' is usually undertaken by a carefully harnessed female model from Mestre on the opening day of Carnival.

It seems that this practice began in 1548 when, on the Thursday before Lent, a Turk using a long balancing-rod had ascended the tower on a tightrope from an anchored boat. But the Venetians outdid their eternal enemies with 'flights' performed by artistes from the Arsenale, by seamen and by gondoliers. In 1680 a man called Scartenador ascended from the water to the bells on horseback; then, on foot, he climbed to the angel at the top, ended up on the halo and waved a flag. That same year, Giovanni Bajo, from a family of belfry climbers, went up the tower to perform acrobatics on the carved lion. He did two handstands, then lost his balance and fell, crashing down to the paving stones below.

Galileo first demonstrated the telescope to Venetian noblemen from the Campanile, and Goethe at the age of thirty-seven saw the sea for the first time from it. In 1902 it collapsed. This symbol of the city could not be allowed to disappear. It was rebuilt at once *com'era e dov'era* – as it was and where it was.

tourism on the Lido, projects for doubling the size of the bridge over the lagoon, public transport by *vaporetto* (steam-boat) and the municipalization of gas, electricity and water supplies, using private capital from the Veneto, elsewhere in Italy and abroad.

Culture gradually revived, along with the economy. In 1895 the first International Art Exhibition, later called the Biennale, was inaugurated and this, with the Teatro La Fenice, which had already premiered operas by Verdi, Rossini, Bellini and Donizetti, gave the city a renewed cultural standing in Europe. The following year the Lumière brothers, pioneers of motion pictures, brought their 'apparatus' to Venice and put on a show at the Teatro Minerva in San Moise. The *Gazzetta di Venezia* reported: 'Imagine watching a scene of any kind, and imagine seeing it reproduced by projection on to a cloth with all the movements, shadows and attitudes that are appropriate to it; were it not for the absence of sound, the illusion would be complete.' New modes of communication were changing the whole world.

While, on the political front, the radicals were about to join forces with the socialists in Venice, visitors continued to arrive from all over the world. These included Henry James, who frequented an exclusive club of

Above: Bathing huts on the Lido.
Opposite: The distinctive Campanile of St Mark's can be seen from the remotest parts of the city.

BARON CORVO: NOVELIST AND SEX TOURIST

LICENTIOUSNESS AND DEPRAVITY – Byron, Casanova, all those monks and nuns whose cloistered lives owed more to carnal lust than to spiritual fulfilment – have frequently been associated with Venice. At the beginning of the twentieth century another joined their ranks: he was an eccentric failed priest named Frederick William Rolfe, who liked to be known as Baron Corvo.

A victim of his indulgent personality, Rolfe was driven by self-destructive urges, a sense of guilt at being homosexual, and utter narcissism. His works reflect his character: unrestrained praise of himself and a torrent of vicious spite directed at friends and acquaintances, who he felt had all betrayed him. He sought success, but all he did prevented it ever coming.

Rolfe's admiration of the beauty of young Venetian boys was sincere, and

he was one of the very few foreigners of the time to be perfectly frank about the poverty that made them so easily available. His *Venice Letters* are a blunt, at times merciless, description of what amounted to homosexual tourism. In his novel *The Desire and Pursuit of the Whole: A Romance of Modern Venice*, he describes his

Venetian years with pleasure and in poetic terms, but also with extraordinary envy:

Young Venice has as superb a physique as can be found anywhere. In a city where everyone swims from his cradle and almost everyone above five years old has rowed … for twenty or thirty generations … you may see (without search) the keen, prompt, level eyes, the noble firm necks, the opulent shoulders, the stalwart arms, the utterly magnificent breasts, the lithely muscular bodies inserted in (and springing from) the well-compacted hips, the long, slim, sinewy-rounded legs, the large, agile, sensible feet of that immortal youth to which Hellas once gave diadems.

Rolfe lurched from a life of *fin-de-siècle* decadence to abject poverty, and he sponged on his friends – with whom he soon quarrelled anyway – in order to pay his bills. Embittered and paranoid to the last, he died of heart failure in Venice in 1913.

Above: Caricatures of nineteenth-century visitors to Venice.

travelling aesthetes, artists and literati, and an Englishman, the self-styled Baron Corvo who, to make ends meet, introduced compliant Venetian lads to wealthy English merchants (see above).

During the mid-nineteenth century the USA discovered Venice: wealthy American citizens did the fashionable thing and rented palazzi, where they entertained lavishly, often surrounding themselves with a coterie of their artistic compatriots. Henry James, born in New York in 1843, was among the best known of the latter. A fortuitous accident rendered him unfit for military service in his homeland's Civil War, and he began to publish reviews, critical essays and stories. In 1869 the young James arrived in Europe, to which he had always been drawn. His first works written here consisted of travel notes documenting the impact that Europe had made on him.

The influence of Venice can be clearly seen in his novel *The Aspern Papers* (1888). One of its characters is based on Mrs Arthur Bronson, a rich American lady who also befriended Robert Browning and lived in the magnificent Palazzo Giustiniani-Recanati on the Grand Canal. The theme of the novel is literature, but the story unfolds in Venice and was inspired by an anecdote concerning the efforts of an American sea captain to gain possession of some mysterious documents by Shelley from one of Byron's lovers, the elderly Clare Clairmont, in Florence. The story is narrated by a young scholar who paints a fine picture of the city:

I don't know why it happened that on this occasion I was more than ever struck with that queer air of sociability, of cousinship and family life, which makes up half the expression of Venice. Without streets and vehicles, the uproar of wheels, the brutality of horses, and with its little winding ways where people crowd together, where voices sound as in the corridors of a house, where the human step circulates as if it skirted the angles of furniture and shoes never wear out, the place has the character of an immense collective apartment, in which Piazza San Marco is the most ornamented corner … and palaces and churches, for the rest, play the part of great divans of repose, tables of entertainment, expanses of decoration. And somehow the splendid common domicile, familiar, domestic and resonant, also resembles a theatre, with actors clicking over bridges and, in straggling processions, tripping along fondamentas … As you sit in your gondola the footways that in certain parts edge the canals assume to the eye the importance of a stage, meeting it at the same angle, and the Venetian figures, moving to and fro against the battered scenery of their little houses of comedy, strike you as members of an endless dramatic troupe.

James and the society painter John Singer Sargent were often guests of the Curtis family, American patrons who loved the lagoon and surrounded themselves with artists and writers in the Gothic Palazzo Barbaro, one of the most splendid palaces in the city. It was adorned inside with

Below: The baroque façade of the church of San Stae, painted by John Singer Sargent in 1913. The goldsmiths' guild is next door.

eighteenth-century paintings and decorations and it featured in James's novel *The Wings of the Dove* (1902). In one of his letters he recalls having slept 'in that divine old library … [gazing] upward from [the] couch, in the rosy dawn, or during the postprandial (that is after-luncheon) siesta, at the medallions and arabesques of the ceiling … '

THE FIRST WORLD WAR: BOMBS FALL ON VENICE

In the early years of the twentieth century Venice began to recover its equilibrium, thanks to a constructive administration that supported the Biennale and the major cultural centres, such as the fine arts academy, the university and the conservatoire. But just when the city seemed poised for further progress, everything was brought to a shuddering halt.

The opening shots of the First World War were fired in Sarajevo on 28 June 1914, when a young Serb nationalist assassinated Archduke Franz Ferdinand, heir to the Hapsburg throne of Austria, and his wife. Europe lined up according to ententes made in the previous years: the Allies, consisting of Britain, France, Russia and Serbia, against the Central Powers of Germany, the Austro-Hungarian Empire and the Ottoman Turkish Empire. Other countries joined, on both sides, as the war dragged on. Italy was at first one of those that remained neutral – but not so its citizen Benito Mussolini, who was already becoming a force to be reckoned with. Fanatical nationalist groups were being financed by France, which had given Mussolini large sums of money to mount an interventionist campaign to broaden the battle fronts and thus, it was hoped, to halt the German army. On the eve of Italy's entry into the war on the Allied side in 1915, it was promised various territories currently in the hands of the enemy: Trentino-Alto-Adige, Trieste, Istria and the Dalmatian islands from Austria, together with a port in Turkey.

Trench warfare characterized the conflict, with asphyx-iating gas attacks and frequent desertions: the Italians and Austrians slaughtered each other in their thousands up in the mountains, less than 50 kilometres (31 miles) from St Mark's Square. So when the Italian troops were crushed at Caporetto in 1917, Venice became victim to heavy air attacks. One hundred thousand people hurriedly left the lagoon. The most destructive of the Austrian bombs fell near the railway station and destroyed the ceiling of the church of the Scalzi, which was decorated with frescoes by Tiepolo depicting Christ's Agony in the Garden. ' "*Non passa lo straniero,*" *il Piave mormorò*' – ' "The foreigner shall not pass," whispered the Piave' was the fervent hope of all Venetians and the Austrians were indeed halted at the River Piave. It was graffittied by a soldier on the walls of a house near his base.

With the coming of peace, many major projects were revived. In 1917 the industrial district at Porto Marghera, the brainchild of the entrepreneur Giuseppe Volpi and a number of similarly minded businessmen, had been inaugurated; it was to expand throughout the 1920s and 1930s and especially in the decades after the Second World War, when it mushroomed to become one of the largest industrial zones in Europe, well serviced via the port development, railway and road infrastructures. The scheme was driven by the opportunity to use the low-cost labour of farm workers in the vicinity. Awareness of the delicacy of Venice's natural environment to industrial pollution, on which the life of the city depends, had yet to emerge.

Fascism was imposed nationwide when Mussolini became Prime Minister in 1922, and dictator, known as *Il Duce* (the Leader), three years later. As with many other regimes led by a powerful and charismatic personality, Mussolini's could be said to have started well. Law and order and public works were high on the list of priorities. The energetic Giuseppe Volpi, who did so much to revive Venice's status as a commercial force, was an early supporter and held office in Mussolini's government. the loss of personal freedom under an ideology in which the needs and desires of the individual were always subordinated to those of the State was a high price for the Italian people to pay. The Fascists swept away all other political parties and labour organizations, including those of Catholic inspiration that had solid roots in the Veneto. Political movements in Venice itself were also thrown into confusion, although there were cells of active anti-Fascists, many of whom were persecuted.

Italy did not escape the Great Depression of the 1930s, and the situation was aggravated by the economic sanctions imposed by the League of Nations in response to the war in East Africa. As Italy had acquired Libya and Tripolitania from the decaying Ottoman Empire just before the First World War, Mussolini subsequently tried to increase Italy's colonial presence in Africa. In the 1930s he had cast an eye on Abyssinia (now Ethiopia), where a previous invasion in the late nineteenth century had ended in a bloody, humiliating defeat at the hands of native tribesmen This time the outcome was reversed.

Italy, since 1936 Germany's ally in the Axis Pact, entered the Second World War in 1940. At this time most of Europe had been over-run by the German army, and Britain seemed to be on the cusp of invasion. However, the speedy victory that Hitler envisaged was not achieved, and Italian troops went on to fight in France, Greece, the Balkans, North Africa and Russia. Fortunately, this time Venice itself was treated with some clemency – the city was spared the air-raids that hammered nearby industrial towns, including Mestre and Marghera.

THE BEST AIR-RAID SHELTER IN TOWN

———

DURING THE WARS of independence and the First and Second World Wars, the palace that my family bought in 1919 was considered the most solidly built in the neighbourhood. It therefore became the local place of refuge, and later the air-raid shelter, with fresh water provided by the well in its entrance hall.

The owners of the palace since the 1700s had been the Baglioni family, a publishing dynasty specializing in religious books. They all fled the city during the Austrian bombardments of 1848, and again in 1917–18 when they left an old soldier as caretaker. He was on his own and, to amuse himself, would fire off his pistol at the figures in the ceiling frescoes.

of human happiness that passes unconsciously into eternal bliss. But the Endymion of the Palazzo Baglioni must have been woken and rendered mortal, if not by the innumerable air-raids of the First World War, then certainly by the activities of the eccentric custodian. And about this time the family decided to sell the place.

A few years earlier my grandfather Andrea da Mosto had begun looking for a palace to buy. Then the First World War broke out and he was called up into the artillery, first as a lieutenant and later promoted to captain. Between 1915 and 1918 he received twenty-one postings, and spent most of his time being transferred from one place to another. Demobilized in 1919, he returned to Venice to work in the State Archive, where he later became director and a prolific author and expert on Venetian history. He resumed his search for a palace and began negotiations for the Palazzo Baglioni.

The transaction was a nightmare, not only on account of the trigger-happy custodian but also because ownership was divided among many members of the Baglioni family. Then Andrea had trouble funding the purchase: his late mother's investments had vanished along with the Austro-Hungarian Empire, as had the properties of his aunt, Princess Lobanov de Rostov, in the wake of the Russian Revolution. But by selling

a family villa in Mirano and a chinchilla fur coat, and making a few other transactions, Andrea finally managed to clinch the deal.

This is the palace in which my family now lives, along with thirty or so tenants on the upper floors and artists' studios in the attic. Many films have been shot here, including *Senso* (1953), directed by Luchino Visconti, *Eva* (1962), by Joseph Losey, and Anthony Minghella's *The Talented Mr Ripley* (1999). Today, the eclectic life in the attic studios, frequented by painters, musicians and designers, among others, is as intriguing as the splendours of the *piano nobile*.

His favourite target was a fresco by Francesco Zucchi depicting the goddess Diana and Endymion, a shepherd of rare beauty. According to Greek mythology Zeus allowed Endymion to become immortal and never grow old, immersed in a perpetual sleep. He was the symbol

Left: The *piano nobile* in my family's home, with its eighteenth-century furniture and plasterwork.
Above: Bullet holes mar the raised arm of Diana in this ceiling fresco, inflicted by a trigger-happy custodian in the early twentieth century.

THE LIFE AND DEATH OF THE *ALVISE DA MOSTO*

THE ITALIAN NAVY's *Alvise da Mosto*, named after my illustrious seafaring ancestor, was launched in 1931. A vessel known as a scout-cruiser, later reclassified as a destroyer, it was built for speed and could achieve around 70 kilometres (43½ miles) per hour, then the world record; it still holds the Italian navy speed record today. The invitation to the launching ceremony depicted a seaman holding a bulldog by the tail, symbolizing anti-British sentiments of the day. As she officially launched the ship, my grand-mother Eugenia, no doubt in words written for her by the authorities, expressed a desire that 'if the day of trial comes, may she allow you to add to the glorious exploits of our navy for the good of our King and our country, marching towards ever greater and more radiant destinies under the leadership of Il Duce'.

With the outbreak of war, and in particular the campaign fought between the Italian and British armies in the Western Desert, the day of trial for the *Alvise da Mosto* did indeed come. In October 1941 major British reinforcements arrived in the Mediterranean. Operated out of Malta, they included two fast light cruisers and two destroyers, which, assisted by early radar, launched heavy attacks on the Italian convoys and their destroyer escorts on the Libyan route. That December the *Alvise da Mosto*, commanded by Captain Francesco dell'Anno, was escorting the tanker *Mantovani* to Tripoli when it was attacked by a powerful British force. Dell'Anno employed every possible means of offence and defence to protect the tanker; finally, with his charge hit and still under bombardment, he tried towing it. But the *Alvise da Mosto* itself was then hit in the powder magazine and, with water flooding the deck and the vessel listing fatally, he gave orders to abandon ship. For his bravery he was awarded the Gold Medal for Military Courage.

As a child, I remember attending, with my brother and parents, a mass in the church of San Giorgio Maggiore to commemorate those crew members who were killed. Standing alongside us were the survivors, gathered together to remember their fallen comrades and the glorious end of their ship.

After almost a year and a half of war, Italian operations in North Africa required major reinforcements from the mainland. Troops and equipment were ferried mainly by sea, in merchant ships escorted by destroyers. It was on one such convoy, in December 1941, that the destroyer *Alvise da Mosto* was sunk (see opposite).

In September 1943, by which time Mussolini had been overthrown and the Allies had begun to invade Italy from the south, armistice terms were agreed. German troops flooded into the country in an attempt to repel the invasion. The anti-Fascists now became partisans, fighting a guerrilla war against Italy's former ally. My father, who was then aged nineteen with no particular love for Mussolini, lived through these stirring events. These are his recollections, starting on the day after the armistice when the occupying Germans moved in.

We had the feeling that a mantle of repression and fear would fall on the Italians as we distributed leaflets that the anti-Fascist parties had printed the night before, urging resistance to the Germans. The few people left in the city regarded us with concern and suspicion. Some took a leaflet and read it in silence or, after a fleeting glance, folded it up and put it in their pocket. Many people refused one out of fear – almost apologetically. The limited freedom of the forty-five days after the fall of Fascism on 25 July had ended, and the long period of Nazi-Fascist oppression was looming.

On the morning of 10 September, a German plane flew over the city several times dropping coloured leaflets; we collected as many as we could to destroy them. When I got home, my father, an old anti-Fascist but worried about my safety, begged me not to go out too often for fear of round-ups. It was impossible: politics had got into my blood around the end of 1942 when my brother and I had started discussing with our friends from the Liceo Foscarini [secondary school] the problems the country would be facing after the foreseeable defeat. Our badge of recognition was a tiny lion of St Mark.

Realizing that we were isolated and that we needed to make contact with other groups, we singled out our Italian teacher, Agostino Zanon dal Bo, as a probable opponent of Fascism. After spending several days tossing back and forth among ourselves the responsibility for getting into conversation with him and trying to sound out his political opinions, we drew straws and it fell to Benvenuti. He went along with the excuse of asking some question about his school work, and managed to discover that our teacher was involved with a political organization. We then went back to him together. He talked to us about what needed to be done if Fascism collapsed, gave us books on history and political economy and introduced us to other lads with anti-Fascist ideas. Gradually we got to know the leaders of the Action Party to which Zanon dal Bo belonged and we started reading the first clandestine newspapers, like La Ricostruzione.

Above: A photograph of my father, Ranieri, taken during the Second World War.
Opposite: Marghera, the industrial villain of Venice's living theatre.

All this happened in April 1943; then things started moving fast. In July the Allies invaded Sicily; Mussolini, still at the helm but not for much longer, reshuffled the government; and the opposition political parties came out into the open. Three months later, with a new non-Fascist government about to sign the armistice and the Anglo-American invasion force starting the long and brutal struggle to capture the Italian mainland, Italy's former allies came rolling inexorably down from the Brenner Pass.

The first German units arrived in Venice on 10 September. They took possession of the main strategic points in the city and in the evening began deporting prisoners. These included several hundred young sailors, boys of fourteen or fifteen who had been locked in their barracks by the commander and could not escape. I still remember them singing as they were taken away on two or three tugboats, passing right in front of the railway station at Santa Lucia, unaware that they were going into captivity and that many of them would never return to their families.

The Resistance was already getting organized. Two Action Party workers and some friends managed to get hold of a lot of munitions from a barracks. These were walled up under a staircase in my home, where they remained until 27 April 1945. They then phoned me from a tavern near the Rialto bridge to say that a dozen or so soldiers had left behind some rifles before going away dressed in civilian clothes. They asked me what should be done with them, and I advised them to take them to certain friends of theirs on the Lido who would hide them.

Unfortunately, a couple of months later one lad involved was indiscreet and there was a big round-up. They arrested first Zanon dal Bo, then me – regardless of the fact that my chest was in plaster after an operation on my collar-bone at the end of November – and kept me in the Santa Maria Maggiore prison from around Christmas until early 1944. I was lucky, as were the other patriots in the Venetian prisons, due partly to the German command's efforts to make Venice a kind of open city – which also worked to its own advantage. A German soldier had been killed by a partisan in Venice, I think at the beginning of January, and we could have been shot in reprisal. But the German command insisted he had been killed by one of his fellow soldiers, a Pole, in a quarrel about a woman. And, thanks to that, I am still here to tell my story. However, from then on I was kept under surveillance and could no longer move about freely.

The ranks of young men in the Action Party were swelling. I maintained my contacts, distributing clandestine newssheets and was a skilful forger of 'official documents' for the numerous patriots who did not want to be conscripted into Graziani's [pro-German] army, or who needed to be able to move around to organize the Resistance. I managed to get hold of a hundred-odd provisional discharge papers in April or May 1944 and, thanks to the collaboration of a soldier in the provincial recruiting office, sent about a hundred 'temporarily unfit for duty' forms and rejection forms to the Christian Democrats as well as the Communists.

In the meantime, many young Venetians had gone to the mountains to fight

with the partisans. In the city the round-ups increased and the fighting became
more ruthless, while Venetian citizens endured murderous raids by the Fascist Black
Brigades, full of anger and bitterness. The hated occupation seemed endless, but we
lived in hope.

That hope was justified. In April 1945, with the war clearly lost, Mussolini,
having earlier been sprung from captivity by the Germans who set him
up at the head of a puppet government, attempted to flee to Switzerland.
Captured by the partisans, he was shot along with his mistress Claretta
Petacci. On the same day the Venetian Fascists surrendered to the partisans.
Two days later, Hitler himself committed suicide in Berlin. On 28 April
there was an armed insurrection in Venice, and on the following day the
Allies entered the city to complete the task of liberation. My father recalls:

The British general Bernard Freyberg was unable to accept the idea that the
Americans, who had already liberated Rome, should be the first to arrive in Venice,
so he moved his own New Zealand troops in. Freyberg had a special feeling for
Venice because he had spent his honeymoon here in 1920.

Two or three days afterwards, on behalf of the National Liberation Command,
I escorted some unarmed British officers to certain factories in Marghera in order to
requisition them because they had collaborated with the Germans. I was dressed in
the only dark suit I owned – an evening suit – and carried a machine-gun. The
British asked me for some special documents in order to infiltrate Yugoslavia – during
the war we had become real experts at forgery and developed a reputation for it.

My father remembers the great dignity of the Venetians when it was all
over, and also his own sense of sadness and loss:

When the Germans surrendered they marched along Via Ventidue Marzo and,
despite everything, the people stood in silence, offering no insolence or violence.
These were moments of great emotion, but also of regret at not having done more
in the struggle for liberation, and not being able to remember the names of all those
dear young friends who had given themselves to the Resistance with total dedication
and a pure spirit.

FIRE AND FLOOD

Everyone has always wanted a piece of Venice: more than a century ago,
on one side romantic souls such as Byron and Ruskin wanted to let Venice
crumble. Facing them were the industrialists who wanted to destroy it and
start again. In the middle were we Venetians – trapped between these two
opposing forces, each in their own way self-centred and deeply unrealistic.

Venice was proud of its unique, other-worldly position as a city out of time, and that was the way it wanted to stay; but the outside world was changing. Throughout the 1930s and 1940s it resisted the tireless march towards the future, but the only way for it to survive as a city was for it to grow. So it grew on the mainland, in the form of huge docks and petrochemical processing work – heavy industry all but engulfed the Serenissima. After the Second World War, Marghera and Mestre pursued their own paths of economic and urban development in line with that of the industrial regions of northern Italy, forcing Venice to turn its face towards the mainland.

In 1951 the industrialist Count Vittorio Cini, who had amassed a fortune from the development at Marghera, set up a cultural foundation on the island of San Giorgio in memory of his son Giorgio, who had been killed in a flying accident. This new venture became a centre for artistic experimentation, including the work of the avant-garde composer Luigi Nono.

Nono, born in 1924, studied at the Venice conservatoire and became a leading figure on the European post-war musical scene, experimenting with radically innovative idioms and techniques. He received constant support from the civic authorities; the philosopher and former mayor of Venice, Massimo Cacciari, with whom he collaborated, wrote:

Nono transformed his wide reading – philosophy, theology, essays – into wholly personal musical and literary figures. Similarly with regard to the problem of interpretation: Nono's thinking does not come "before" his compositional work, nor does he supply illustrations afterwards; it coexists with the musical idea, becomes one with the composition itself; it does not exist if not in the concrete dimension of listening.

But innovation and modernization where the fabric of the city was concerned had been insidiously building up problems for the future. Alterations to the lagoon, such as the dredging of a deep channel between Malamocco and Porto Marghera for oil tankers; water pollution from industrial wastewater and agricultural run-off from the catchment area; artificial islands created from draining areas of saltmarsh; together with the establishment of large fish farms, subsidence and increasingly frequent high tides – all these had made the lagoon system more fragile than it had ever been. In the 1960s nature caught up with Venice and dealt the city a terrible blow.

Throughout its sixteen hundred-year existence Venice conquered cities, defended itself and its territories against invasion and defied great tyrants and empires – but nothing had prepared it for what happened on 4 November 1966. Torrential rain and strong winds prevented the morning tide from leaving the lagoon. The afternoon tide then rushed in, causing the city to be flooded to a depth of nearly 2 metres (6½ feet) above normal

water level – the highest floods in Venetian history. Although Venice has always flooded a little with the tides, this was much more than the city could cope with. The water stayed for twenty hours; there was a total electricity blackout and underground oil tanks burst, releasing a thick black sludge. People feared for their lives, although in fact no one died. The ground floor of every house in Venice was full of water. In mine, the water came up to the third step on the main staircase. I can remember how scared I was when, aged five, I was taken down to see it by my mother. It was bizarre, too – a boat floated in through our enormous front door to collect my father for work.

The flood had devastated Venice; and it was in the wake of the flood and the pollution that I grew up. The Venice of my childhood was one of tourist booms and the idea of the sinking city. The flood alerted the world to the precariousness of our city in the modern age: charitable British supporters sent funds through 'Venice in Peril', as did many other groups

Above: The severe floods of 1966 were the worst to hit Venice for nearly a thousand years. The water rose by nearly 2 metres (6½ feet) and lapped high on the columns of the Doge's Palace for two days. It left behind a city desolated by rubble and debris.

Above: At least three or four times a month, especially in autumn and winter, the high tide washes into St Mark's Square, moving tourists and Venetians onto temporary, raised wooden walkways.

from around the world, and special legislation was enacted for Venice, financed by central government. Everyone in the world had – and still has – an opinion about Venice; we Venetians sit in the middle and try to get on with our lives. Somehow the conviction grew that it was only by extraordinary intervention that Venice could be saved. There may be some truth in this, but there is also the risk that other essential aspects of everyday life will be overlooked. So while complicated, mammoth, technologically unprecedented projects were drawn up to control the tidal flows, the decay of the city's fabric continued and the natural resilience of the lagoon continued to deteriorate.

But the saving of Venice in general has been a success. Major public investment, scientific research and new technology are overcoming many of the difficulties. Yet the population of Venice – now less than a third of its size in 1945 – continues to dwindle with a consequent increase in the average age (the highest of any city in Europe); friends I grew up with, and many other Venetians, have left the city. Large numbers of those who still work in Venice have had to move to the mainland because it is more affordable. Tourists are over-running the place, homes are being turned into hotels, and local shops are ceasing to supply the necessities of daily life in favour of souvenirs for tourists. At least the three universities, many public and private libraries, galleries and museums, the Biennale and other foundations and institutions have maintained Venice's leading position in cultural life. But even then, a catastrophic fire in the 1990s destroyed part of the city's cultural heritage. To the casual eye it has been reborn, but the new Fenice does not satisfy all of us (see page 228).

The remaining Venetians are angry people. For hundreds of years we nurtured a resourceful, independent existence on our islands, and now we just want that back. Few old Venetian trades survive. Building gondolas, rowing them, blowing glass and fashioning masks were once essential livelihoods in the economy of a great city; now they merely capitalize on the huge tourist industry. Human interventions on the lagoon have already brought the system close to its limit, causing erosion and increased flooding; the impact of climate change is already beginning to manifest itself in the shape of more frequent storms, stronger winds and unseasonal floods.

We have drifted a long way from the fundamental principles the Serenissima relied on for centuries, whereby rights and responsibilities were directed towards the common good of the city and those who stepped out of line were exiled. Today Venice is the victim of petty power struggles, and seemingly anachronistic engineering solutions, such as an underground railway system (when more efficient boats could achieve the same results), become an arid window display to exploit the image of the city. The situation reminds me of the Futurists in the early 1900s, who believed that Italian art had become stagnant and called for a new art glorifying modern technology, energy and violence. Indeed, for many the only answer was, and is, modernization.

Venice might indeed have rightly resisted modern buildings, but maybe the modern city was born here – Venice is still the most perfect city on earth, totally man-made, yet at one with nature. Its labyrinthine layout makes it seem vast, yet human in scale. It does not have traffic jams. It looks so beautiful that it might be a dream. It is the essence of Venice that makes it work. Its canal network, the way it is planned for pedestrians, the closeness to nature, all contribute to making it a perfect urban experience. It may have resisted the bright modern future, but for me it is a forerunner of the most modern city of all – New York. It has the same sense of proportion, the same mood of an all-encompassing city. I see it as an organism with canal-shaped veins and arteries in which it is difficult to tell where one building stops and the next one ends, the whole 'creature' being greater than the sum of its parts.

TEATRO LA FENICE: A NIGHT LIKE NO OTHER

JUST MARRIED, my wife and I were renting an apartment near the Teatro La Fenice. On 29 January 1996 we had invited some friends over for dinner. Just after the first course, the phone rang: it was the landlord calling to ask me if his house was on fire. From where he was, on the other side of Venice, he could see great clouds of smoke. When I went up on to the *altana* (our wooden roof terrace) I saw to my horror huge flames engulfing the opera house. No one ate much more that evening: we were in the front row of a real drama. We stood there watching,

some crying, some joking to ease the tension, while a helicopter dropped water on to the flames, which were shooting up to twice the height of the surrounding buildings, and we all wondered if the fire would ravage the rest of the city as well.

A sad combination of misdemeanour, bad luck and serious negligence had reduced the Fenice to a great empty shell. It was a calamity for the city, for music lovers around the world and for all Venetians, who had sorrowfully witnessed the destruction of a symbol of their identity. Venice had acquired a wholly new sense of the transience of things. Like the flood of 1966, the Fenice fire severely affected the city's morale. And so, adopting the slogan 'Where it was and as it was',

previously used for the Campanile of St Mark's when it collapsed in 1902, the city authorities and central government immediately began to plan its reconstruction, assisted by many international organizations.

The Fenice has ostensibly been rebuilt now. But despite all the work and money that have gone into the enterprise, and probably on account of the politicians' great haste to finish the task, the new building has something of the computerized mock-up about it, strikingly remote from the traditions and culture that have shaped Venice over the centuries. The reconstruction was delayed for more than five years because of complicated legal issues and planning oversights. Even so, time could surely have been found to ensure that the job was at least carried out properly, especially given the fact that the late architect Aldo Rossi, with whom I worked closely during the competition for the contract to rebuild the Fenice, had created a highly detailed plan of great beauty. To quote one of my mother's sayings: 'The hasty cat has blind kittens.'

Above: The Teatro La Fenice in ruins in 1996. Opposite: Gondoliers are important to tourism and they still run ferry services across the Grand Canal.

No one has given up hope – a constant element in Venetian history, among its highs and lows, splendours and tragedies, has been the ability to emerge triumphant from misfortune and adversity. There is a hope that this unique city will be healed and saved. And maybe this will include a species that otherwise appears to be on its way to extinction: the Venetians themselves.

AN IMAGE OF THE FUTURE

I would not go so far as to say that the bridge between Venice and the mainland should be physically demolished, but the city could at least be virtually separated. To do so would give Venice a chance to rebuild its identity in the third millennium on the same terms as those in which its magnificence originated – protecting it from those who exploit its special status and empowering its remaining citizens to repossess their integrity. As the age of industry draws to a close, a new age of information technology and ecological awareness is emerging – perhaps Venice is once more going to be a place where people can live and work productively.

In the meantime, my family and I spend all our free time on a tiny island in the lagoon, surrounded by marshy wilderness, ignoring the noise of the planes at Marco Polo Airport, seeing and doing what the first settlers in Venice would have seen and done over a thousand years ago. It is not difficult to imagine where Venice could be in the distant future, in a non-industrial world where the fuel supplies have run out and all the cars have rusted away, when mankind has been forced to live on the terms dictated by the natural environment. Even if the city itself no longer exists, by that time the idea of Venice will always endure.

Opposite: Around fifteen million visitors flock to the city every year. Traditional livelihoods and the cultural distinctiveness of Venice are threatened by the intense pressure.
Above: Cruise ships bring the tourists right into the heart of Venice, perhaps endangering fragile infrastructure of the city.
Overleaf: I hope that my city's remarkable history will be preserved along with its monuments, and that a balance can be found between opening its wonders for modern visitors and restoring the integrity and vitality of the Venetian population.

ACKNOWLEDGEMENTS

Above all, I would like to thank my wife Jane for her essential and indispensable help, and, although we never met, my grandfather Andrea, who dedicated himself to Venice and left an incredible amount of writings that took me into the furthest reaches of the long history of the da Mostos; also my parents Ranieri and Maria Grazia, my mother-in-law Victoria Press, my marvellous children Delia, Vettor and Pierangelo, and my brother MarcoAndrea.

Sincere gratitude also to John Parker and June Wallis, Gregory Dowling, David Graham, Emma Shackleton, Linda Blakemore, Sarah Miles, Esther Jagger, Arlene Alexander, Sara Wikner and Deirdre O'Day who all made this book; Jane Root who commissioned the series; and the BBC Arts Features department, associates and crew: Mark Harrison, Basil Comely, Sam Hobkinson, Caroline Lisowicz, Ed Bazalgette, Marco Crivellari, Nina Jaffer, Silvia Sacco, Paul Ralph, Jonathan Furniss, Clare Lewis, Nick Reeks, Chris Hartley, Paul Perryment, Andrea Arnone, Jessie Brough, Fred Fabre, Alex Cooke, Federico Pucci, Johan Perry, Simon Reynell, Anton Jeffes, Mel Quigley, Andrea Carnevale, Eliott McAffrey, Natasha Martin, Jim Spencer, Judith Stanley-Smith, Ged Bryan, Pieter Jurriaanse, Caitlin Tanner, Isobel While, Katy McPhee, Martine Van't Hul, Giorgia Serantoni, Jeff Smart, Peter Salem, Imogen Carter, Mestiere Cinema and Massimo Monico, Daniele and Stefano. I am also grateful to the organizations that occupy and manage all the buildings and precious collections featured in the documentary series and this book, for allowing their able staff to spare the time to give us access.

Many others have also made my work possible: Dan Cruickshank, Caroline Press, Suzanne and Graham Day, Samantha Weinberg and Mark Fletcher, Kim Bevan, Alice Rayman, Giuseppe Baldissera, Giacomo Baldissera, Giorgio Rossini, Gabriella Delfini, Ettore Vio, Janusz Podrazik, Gioia Meller Markowicz, Viola Venturini, Stefano Rogliani, Giovanni Caniato, Lady Frances Clarke, Ivano Turlon, Luigi Fozzati, Sergio Tegon, Fulvio Caputo, Umberto Marcello, Francesca Forni, Comandante Garlisi, Anna Bravetti, Donatella Asta, Giorgio Nubar Gianighian, Girolamo Fazzini, Maria Novella Benzoni, Roberto de Feo, Nino, Mario Costantini, Sr Baradella, Ivano and Emilio, Archivio di Stato and Biblioteca Marciana, Marino Zorzi, Alvise Zorzi, Deborah Howard, the Venetian publishers Filippi, Giuseppe Tassini, Giulio Lorenzetti, i Vittoria, gli Scarpa, the many who have written or write about Venice, and those who still believe in Venice.

A special thanks to the BBC for giving me this opportunity.

INDEX

Below: An amazing view of the city at dawn with the Dolomites behind. Due to pollution and low cloud, the mountains are rarely seen so clearly.

CREDITS

BBC Books would like to thank the following for providing photographs and for permission to reproduce copyright material. While every effort has been made to trace and acknowledge copyright holders, we would like to apologize should there have been any errors or omissions.

All of the photographs in this book are © John Parker with the exception of:
Endpapers: Museo Correr/SCALA; page 33 top Galleria dell'Accademia, Venice/SCALA; 33 below Museo Correr/SCALA; 34 Museo Correr/SCALA; 75 Collezione Crespi, Milano/SCALA; 76 Museum of Fine Arts, Boston/Bridgeman Art Library; 77 Galleria dell'Accademia, Venice/Bridgeman Art Library; 83 Galleria d'Arte Moderna, Venezia/ SCALA; 88 (detail) Fondazione Querini Stampalia, Venezia/Art Archive; 94 Fotomas Index; 96 National Gallery London/Bridgeman Art Library; 99 (detail) Museo Correr/ Bridgeman Art Library; 127 Birmingham Museums & Art Gallery; 155 Galleria Nazionale d'Arte Antica/SCALA; 178 Ca' Rezzonico, Museo del Settecento/Bridgeman Art Library; 183 Private Collection/ Bridgeman Art Library; 194 Private Collection/ Bridgeman Art Library; 203 Topham/AP
Images on the following pages were supplied by the author:
37, 73, 148, 185 and 201
We would also like to acknowledge the following for authorizing the reproduction of images of various public sites in Venice, and to thank them for their co-operation and assistance:
Museo Navale Arsenale; Fondazione Giorgio Cini; Museo Correr; Ufficio Beni Culturali, Sezione Beni Artistici, Storici e Museali; Ufficio Beni Culturali del Patriarcato di Venezia (churches);
La Comunità Ebraica di Venezia; Ufficio Marketing dei Civici Musei; Direzione Palazzo Ducale; Soprintendenza di Venezia e Laguna di Venezia

The quotations on pages 15 and 159 have been taken from the following books: page 15; *Venice: The Rise to Empire* by John Julius Norwich (1977), Allen Lane; page 159; *Storia della musica sacra nella già Capella ducale di S. Marco in Venezia, dal 1318 al 1797* by Francesco Caffi (1987) Olschki, Firenze

All imperial equivalents are approximate and no equivalent for metric tonnes has been given. One short ton (US) is equivalent to 0.907 metric tonnes.

This book is published to accompany the television series entitled
Francesco's Venice, first broadcast on BBC2 in 2004.
Executive producer: Basil Comely Series producer: Sam Hobkinson

10 9 8 7 6 5 4 3 2 1

First published in hardback in 2004.
This paperback edition published in 2007 by BBC Books,
an imprint of Ebury Publishing
Ebury Publishing is a division of the Random House Group

The Random House Group Limited Reg. No. 954009
Addresses for companies within the Random House Group can be found at
www.randomhouse.co.uk

A CIP catalogue record for this book is available from the British Library
The Random House Group Limited makes every effort to ensure that the
papers used in our books are made from trees that have been legally
sourced from well-managed and credibly certified forests. Our paper
procurement policy can be found at www.randomhouse.co.uk

Printed and bound in China by C&C Offset Printing Co.,Ltd

ISBN 978 0 563 49363 1

Commissioning Editor: Emma Shackleton
Project Editor: Sarah Reece
Copy Editor: Esther Jagger
Translators: Gregory Dowling and David Graham
Art Director and Designer: Linda Blakemore
Picture Researcher: Deirdre O'Day
Production Controller: Peter Hunt